As the Lilacs Bloomed

D0052268

THE AZRIELI SERIES OF HOLOCAUST SURVIVOR MEMOIRS: PREVIOUSLY PUBLISHED TITLES

ENGLISH TITLES

Album of My Life by Ann Szedlecki

Bits and Pieces by Henia Reinhartz

A Drastic Turn of Destiny by Fred Mann

E/96: Fate Undecided by Paul-Henri Rips

Fleeing from the Hunter by Marian Domanski

From Generation to Generation by Agnes Tomasov

Gatehouse to Hell by Felix Opatowski

Getting Out Alive by Tommy Dick

If, By Miracle by Michael Kutz

If Home Is Not Here by Max Bornstein

If Only It Were Fiction by Elsa Thon

In Hiding by Marguerite Élias Quddus

Knocking on Every Door by Anka Voticky

Little Girl Lost by Betty Rich

Memories from the Abyss by William Tannenzapf/ *But I Had a Happy Childhood* by Renate Krakauer

The Shadows Behind Me by Willie Sterner

Spring's End by John Freund

Suddenly the Shadow Fell by Leslie Meisels with Eva Meisels

Survival Kit by Zuzana Sermer

Tenuous Threads by Judy Abrams/ *One of the Lucky Ones* by Eva Felsenburg Marx

Under the Yellow and Red Stars by Alex Levin

Vanished Boyhood by George Stern

The Violin by Rachel Shtibel/ *A Child's Testimony* by Adam Shtibel

W Hour by Arthur Ney

We Sang in Hushed Voices by Helena Jockel

As the Lilacs Bloomed
Anna Molnár Hegedűs

First published as *Miért?* (Why?) in Romania, 1946.

TRANSLATED FROM HUNGARIAN
BY MARIETTA MORRY AND LYNDA MUIR

FIRST EDITION
Copyright © 2014 The Azrieli Foundation and others

All rights reserved

Copyright in individual works, parts of works and/or photographs included within this published work is also claimed by individuals and entities. All requests and questions concerning copyright and reproduction of all or part of this publication may be directed to The Azrieli Foundation.

THE AZRIELI FOUNDATION
www.azrielifoundation.org

Cover and book design by Mark Goldstein
Endpaper maps by Martin Gilbert
Map on page xxix by François Blanc

LIBRARY AND ARCHIVES CANADA CATALOGUING IN PUBLICATION

Hegedüsné Molnár, Anna
[Miért? English]
    As the lilacs bloomed / Anna Molnár Hegedüs; translated from Hungarian by Marietta Morry and Lynda Muir.

(The Azrieli series of Holocaust survivor memoirs. VI)
Translation of: Miért?
Includes bibliographical references and index.
ISBN 978-1-897470-48-0 (pbk.)

1. Hegedüsné Molnár, Anna. 2. Jews – Romania – Satu Mare – Biography. 3. Holocaust, Jewish (1939–1945) – Romania – Satu Mare – Personal narratives. 4. Holocaust survivors – Canada – Biography. I. Azrieli Foundation, issuing body II. Title. III. Title: Miért? English. IV. Series: Azrieli series of Holocaust survivor memoirs. Series VI

DS135.R73H44 2014   940.53'18092   C2014-906278-8

MIX
From responsible sources
FSC   FSC® C004191
www.fsc.org

PRINTED IN CANADA

The Azrieli Series of Holocaust Survivor Memoirs

Naomi Azrieli, Publisher

Jody Spiegel, Program Director
Arielle Berger, Managing Editor
Elizabeth Lasserre, Senior Editor, French-Language Editions
Aurélien Bonin, French-Language Educational Outreach and Events
Catherine Person, Quebec Educational Outreach and Events
Elin Beaumont, English-Language Educational Outreach and Events
Tim MacKay, New Media and Marketing

Susan Roitman, Executive Assistant and Office Manager (Toronto)
Mary Mellas, Executive Assistant and Human Resources (Montreal)
Eric Bélisle, Administrative Assistant

Mark Goldstein, Art Director
François Blanc, Cartographer
Bruno Paradis, Layout, French-Language Editions

Contents

Series Preface:
In their own words...

In telling these stories, the writers have liberated themselves. For so many years we did not speak about it, even when we became free people living in a free society. Now, when at last we are writing about what happened to us in this dark period of history, knowing that our stories will be read and live on, it is possible for us to feel truly free. These unique historical documents put a face on what was lost, and allow readers to grasp the enormity of what happened to six million Jews – one story at a time.

David J. Azrieli, C.M., C.Q., M.Arch
Holocaust survivor and founder, The Azrieli Foundation

Since the end of World War II, over 30,000 Jewish Holocaust survivors have immigrated to Canada. Who they are, where they came from, what they experienced and how they built new lives for themselves and their families are important parts of our Canadian heritage. The Azrieli Foundation's Holocaust Survivor Memoirs Program was established to preserve and share the memoirs written by those who survived the twentieth-century Nazi genocide of the Jews of Europe and later made their way to Canada. The program is guided by the conviction that each survivor of the Holocaust has a remarkable story to tell, and that such stories play an important role in education about tolerance and diversity.

Millions of individual stories are lost to us forever. By preserving the stories written by survivors and making them widely available to a broad audience, the Azrieli Foundation's Holocaust Survivor Memoirs Program seeks to sustain the memory of all those who perished at the hands of hatred, abetted by indifference and apathy. The personal accounts of those who survived against all odds are as different as the people who wrote them, but all demonstrate the courage, strength, wit and luck that it took to prevail and survive in such terrible adversity. The memoirs are also moving tributes to people – strangers and friends – who risked their lives to help others, and who, through acts of kindness and decency in the darkest of moments, frequently helped the persecuted maintain faith in humanity and courage to endure. These accounts offer inspiration to all, as does the survivors' desire to share their experiences so that new generations can learn from them.

The Holocaust Survivor Memoirs Program collects, archives and publishes these distinctive records and the print editions are available free of charge to libraries, educational institutions and Holocaust-education programs across Canada. They are also available for sale to the general public at bookstores. All revenues to the Azrieli Foundation from the sales of the Azrieli Series of Holocaust Survivor Memoirs go toward the publishing and educational work of the memoirs program.

The Azrieli Foundation would like to express appreciation to the following people for their invaluable efforts in producing this book: Sherry Dodson (Maracle Press), Sir Martin Gilbert, Steve Jobbitt, Barbara Kamieński, Farla Klaiman, Therese Parent, and Margie Wolfe and Emma Rodgers of Second Story Press.

About the Glossary

The following memoir contains a number of terms, concepts and historical references that may be unfamiliar to the reader. For information on major organizations; significant historical events and people; geographical locations; religious and cultural terms; and foreign-language words and expressions that will help give context and background to the events described in the text, please see the glossary beginning on page 187.

Introduction

The sweet smell of flowers, their intense colour and liveliness, are often cause to rejoice after the winter months, along with the rejuvenation of life. "In the wonderfully fair month of May," wrote Heinrich Heine, "as all the flower-buds burst, then in my heart, love arose." [1]

"I am alive! The lilacs are in bloom again." So writes Anna Molnár Hegedűs on May 1, 1945, just days after returning home to Szatmár, Hungary following horrifying experiences in the Nazi camps. "There was springtime last year as well," she continues, "but we had no eyes for beauty. Our noses could only perceive the stench of human cruelty. Our lips forgot how to smile; our hearts ached." Anna Molnár Hegedűs, like so many others, came to the end of the Holocaust alive but crushed in spirit. Wondering if the Nazis had succeeded in destroying humanity, she is nonetheless struck by the fact that the lilacs never stopped blooming, just as the cycle of the rising sun and moon were constantly in motion. Other people did not stop living, children did not cease being born and parents did not stop looking with wonder at their first smile. "I am alive," Anna writes, "and I can take delight in this new spring." But this return to life is conditional: If her loved ones do not return, she will feel "sentenced to life."

---

1 Heinrich Heine, 1840: Im wunderschönen Monat Mai, Als alle Knospen sprangen, Da ist in meinem Herzen Die Liebe aufgegangen.

Anna set her memoirs to paper in 1945, pouring them out in the months following liberation. Her memoir was originally published in Hungarian in 1946. Written without the hindsight and processing that characterizes most survivor memoirs, Anna plunges the reader into a harsh and unsettling present. The reader moves along with Anna, day after day, experiencing, as she did, the German invasion of Hungary in March 1944, the anti-Jewish decrees, the ghetto and the horror of the camps. On March 19, 1944, the start of the occupation, Anna Hegedűs was forty-seven years old and staying in a spa-hotel in Budapest for treatment for her sciatica. The news of the occupation left her in shock, and Anna eloquently shares this bewilderment with the reader. When Anna returns to Szatmár, her story of survival begins: the anxieties and ideas for escape, the concern for her family, the imprisonment in the ghetto and deportation to Auschwitz-Birkenau, the transfer to Schlesiersee labour camp, the "death march," the liberation and the anticipation of the return of her family. Ending her narrative at this point, Anna is not an all-knowing storyteller; the end is unresolved, as it was for her at the time. This anxiety of "not-knowing" the ending of her story embraces the reader as well.

Anna Hegedűs was born in 1897 in a city called Satmar in Yiddish, Satu Mare in Romanian and Szatmárnémeti in Hungarian. Anna was the youngest daughter of Henrik Molnár and Fanny Moskovits. She had two brothers, Lászlo and Ödön, and three sisters, Margit (who died before the war), Iren and Erzsike. She married Zoltán Hegedűs in 1921 and two years later their daughter, Ágnes, was born, followed by their son, János, in 1927.

Szatmár, situated in north Transylvania, was the largest city in Satu Mare County and was founded in the twelfth century by German settlers. The first evidence of the presence of Jews in the city is from 1698, and from then on many Jews resided there, suffering over the years from various restrictions regarding their rights to settlement and trade. Nonetheless, a Jewish community was established and by

1941, the year of the last national Hungarian census held before the German occupation, 12,960 Jews lived there, comprising a quarter of its population. Most of them were traders and craftsmen, but there were also factory owners – Anna's husband managed a lumber-processing factory – and farmers who employed mainly Jewish workers. The city had two Jewish schools, a parochial primary Talmud Torah school, a yeshiva and various religious and social organizations, and was comprised of an Orthodox community and a "status quo," or independent, community. According to a census taken after the German occupation, on the second week of April 1944, about 12,000 Jews belonged to the Orthodox community and about 750 belonged to the "status quo" community. At the end of the nineteenth century, the Orthodox community became central to the Hasidic movement in Hungary when Rabbi Joel Teitelbaum founded and established the Satmar sect. Zionism, and particularly religious Zionism, took hold as a movement in the city during the 1930s.

The geo-political status of the city changed over time. Before World War I, Szatmár was part of Hungary; after the war, it was annexed to Romania. Following the Second Vienna Award on August 30, 1940, the borders between Hungary and Romania were re-assigned and a large part of Transylvania was transferred to Hungarian authority. The Jews of north Transylvania, including Szatmár, were once again under Hungarian sovereignty.

After the declaration of the Vienna Award, Romanian soldiers went on a rampage through the city, attacking many Jewish citizens. With the return of Hungarian sovereignty, anti-Jewish legislation that had been established throughout Hungary was now enforced in the region more strictly than in Hungary itself. During the summer of 1941, the Hungarian authorities exiled many Jewish families who couldn't prove Hungarian citizenship – among them about a thousand Jews from Szatmár – to Nazi-occupied Kamenets-Podolsk in the Ukraine. The exiled Jews were murdered there on August 27 or 28. In

1942, most Jewish men were enlisted for forced labour service by the Hungarian army and stationed on the eastern front in the Ukraine, where approximately 42,000 died or were murdered.

Despite the anti-Jewish decrees in Hungary, the exile and the tens of thousands of men enlisted to the forced labour service, the full force of the Nazis' systematic Jewish genocide hit Hungary only after the Nazi occupation. The Jewish population was overwhelmed; within a year, approximately 565,000 Hungarian Jews were murdered, more than 360,000 in Auschwitz.

When the German army invaded Hungary on March 19, 1944, the Hungarian administration was still in place. Under the authority of laws and decrees issued by the central and local Hungarian government authorities, the Jews residing outside of Budapest were soon rounded up into ghettos and, in collaboration with the Nazis, eventually deported. Within three days of the establishment of the Szatmár ghetto on May 3, 1944, about 17,000 Jews were transferred to the ghetto and thoroughly searched for valuables upon entrance. On May 13, 1944, 2,000 Jews were transferred to the Szatmár ghetto from the Nagykároly ghetto, adding to the severe overcrowding: each person was accorded only slightly more than half a metre of floor space. The use of beds was forbidden and the ghetto residents had to sleep on mattresses or straw mattresses. The commander of the ghetto, Hungarian police officer Béla Sárközi, was referred to by the ghetto occupants as "Hitler the second." He personally supervised the torture of Jews, intending to reveal where valuables were hidden. Some of the detainees died as a result of the torture; others, as Anna mentions in her memoir, committed suicide in order to avoid it. Between May 19 and June 1, 1944, 18,863 of the ghetto inhabitants were deported to Auschwitz on six transports. Most of them did not survive.[2]

The vast majority of those who did survive Auschwitz could not

---

2   G. Miron, Ed., S. Shulhani, Co-editor, *The Yad Vashem Encyclopedia of the Ghettos During the Holocaust*. Jerusalem: Yad Vashem, 2010.

write during their imprisonment. It was forbidden to get hold of paper and writing tools. And even if they somehow could, when and where could they have written? And who among them was capable or had the strength? Of the few who did manage to write something while in the camp, most did not survive. The first written testimonies and books about life in the camp began to appear soon after the war's end. Most were in the writer's mother tongue – Polish, Yiddish, Italian, French and German – and were not translated until years later. These individual voices – dozens of books and thousands of testimonies – constitute the initial corpus that began to establish the first voice of the Holocaust, the experiences of the people who lived through it and came back to testify right away. The words of those who did not return were silenced forever.

Anna Molnár Hegedűs's book is part of this corpus of biographical literature written between 1945 and 1948. An important, engaging and stirring book, it joins these early memoirs, all unique, historical sources that constructed initial perspectives on the Holocaust. As opposed to the widespread view that these early memoirs were written exclusively by men, and in the almost complete absence of women from the historiography of the Holocaust in the decades following the war, a relatively considerable number of testimonies and memoirs by women were published immediately after the war. Despite this, the books written by men came to constitute the historiographic base for Holocaust research, and thus established the foundation of the collective memory about the Holocaust.

Besides the inevitable differences among the different writers and those giving testimony, such as their sensitivity, their ability to assess the situation, their language and their biography, we can find important similarities in the wave of publications between 1945 and 1948. In them, the traumas, the challenges and the abuses appear in a far more blatant and less "literary" manner than in later writings. Their experiences and sufferings are described laconically, ostensibly emotionally very "flat," lacking what could be called "philosophical

musings." They lack, almost completely, interpretations of the significance of the evil, of the banality, and of other psychological issues.
The stories were told "as they are."

Survivors wrote under the impact of the first shock and *tabula
rasa*, that is to say, mostly without having read other memoirs or
testimonies. In other words, these early writings were almost unin-
fluenced by the way in which Holocaust memory was shaped, or the
"accepted" way of talking or telling about the Holocaust in later years.
These survivors, so close to the events, were not exposed to the social
influence arising from various opinions and reactions that appeared
after the war, as the writers of later memoirs were. Thus, for example,
we find that the people who appear in this corpus were less exposed
to the concept of "like sheep to the slaughter" – Jewish helplessness
that characterized a certain interpretation prevalent for a time – or to
accusations regarding the use of feminine sexuality for the purpose
of survival, as well as a variety of other accusations that were hurled
at the survivors.

A further prominent characteristic that can be discerned in this
early work is the survivors' terrible loneliness and their lack of knowledge concerning their loved ones' fate and the future in general. As
Anna Hegedűs wrote, "If they don't come home, if I wait in vain and
I can no longer hope, then there will never be spring again and the
lilacs will bloom only over my grave, over my shattered heart." Her
words still lack the conclusiveness of knowing; they are drenched
with the unknown.

There are other parameters involved in early testimony, aside
from the freshness of memory, cases in which the survivors needed to
"distance themselves" in order to be able to speak or write about their
experiences. Primo Levi's words are relevant here: "It is natural that
the most substantial material for the reconstruction of truth about
the camps is constituted by the memories of the survivors. Beyond
the pity and the indignation they arouse, they should be read with
a critical eye. For knowledge of the Lagers, the Lagers themselves

were not always a good observation post. In the inhuman conditions to which they were subjected, the prisoners could barely acquire an overall vision of the universe."[3]

In this context, we always have to recall whose memories we are examining and ask ourselves: What was their gender? When did they arrive at the camp? What were their roles in the camp? Auschwitz, after all, was many places. In many respects it is difficult to speak about the same "Auschwitz" for more than two or three people. The experience of Auschwitz was different from man to woman and from woman to adolescent. Experience depended on the season the prisoner arrived in, the daily "death quota," and the mood of the SS guards. Survival in the camp was a complex patchwork of a variety of factors. The age of a prisoner influenced their experience of Auschwitz in general and influenced their lives in particular. Family status was also a critical characteristic, as was nationality. And, of course, luck was a factor.

Recent studies conclude that approximately 424,000 Hungarian Jews were deported to Auschwitz between May and July 1944. After the selections, about 52,000 men and a similar number of women entered the camp as prisoners. Only 25,000 to 30,000 women were registered as camp inmates – about 25,000 women soon died as a result of the camp conditions or were murdered as a result of the selections. During the following months and until the camp's evacuation in January 1945, between 45,000 and 50,000 prisoners were sent to other camps in Germany. This would mean that some 325,000 to 330,000 Hungarian Jews were killed in the gas chambers directly after their arrival to the camp.[4] Anna Hegedűs was one of the Jewish women who, together with her daughter, Ágnes, entered Auschwitz as prisoner and, after four months, was sent to a forced labour camp.

---

3 P. Levi, *The Drowned and the Saved*. New York: Vintage Books, 1989, p. 16.
4 Auschwitz-Birkenau State Museum

Anna's experience in Auschwitz and other camps was unique and yet shares similarities to others who were on a similar path. Objectively, and generally speaking, all prisoners experienced the same conditions: the terrible loss, proximity to cruelty and death, hunger, cold, humiliation and fear of the unknown; subjectively, each person's experience depended on personality, nationality, date of arrival, family construct, age and gender. For example, Anna offers a fascinating window into the complex relations between the Hungarian Jews and the Slovakian Jews who started arriving in Auschwitz in March 1942. Most Slovakian Jews were murdered, but some of those who survived became prisoners who were given relatively powerful positions in the camp, such as barracks supervisors. In this case, many sources are contradictory. As Yehoshua Büchler states, one can even find that: "In the same source, Slovakian women are described in a very different light [...] Thus, that same *Blockälteste* described in one testimony as collaborating with the SS doctor may be described in another survivor testimony as a savior figure to whom many prisoners owe their lives."[5]

Since the mid-1980s, thanks to researchers in the field, we are now aware of the distinctions between the way that men and women experienced the Holocaust. The female experience was influenced by three main characteristics: Nazi worldview, female physiology, and cultural gender-related characteristics pertaining to the way women experience their lives and the way they remember, write and assign meaning to their experiences. In other words, even when men and women experience what seem to be similar circumstances, they remember, recount, write and assign meaning in different ways.

As the Lilacs Bloomed makes it clear that gender mattered in the Holocaust. Anna discusses at length the fear of sexual assault or abuse of her daughter in the ghetto and in the camps, and describes inci-

---

5   Y. Büchler, "The First in the Killing Fields: Slovakian Jewish Women in Auschwitz 1942," *Moreshet*, 58, 1994, p. 31. [Hebrew]

dents of abuse in both the ghetto and in Auschwitz. Anna recounts instances of "sex for food" – the practice whereby prisoners – mostly Jewish female prisoners who were at the bottom of the prisoner hierarchy – had to engage in sex with prominent prisoners, mainly Poles, to receive additional food that was essential to survival. Many early testimonies and memoirs contain references to "sex for food" whereas, for reasons related to trauma and the ways in which Holocaust memory was shaped during the years, this is not often mentioned in later survivor literature. She also extensively and engagingly discusses the interrelations between female prisoners. It is striking that upon entering the camp, women remained in a purely female world. Encounters with men – SS guards, various functionaries and, rarely, a glimpse of family members – were sporadic.

The touching relationship between Anna and her daughter, Ágnes, was central to her experience of survival. Upon arrival at Auschwitz men and women were separated, and Anna's husband and son were sent to the men's camp while she and her daughter were imprisoned along with one of her nieces. It was not common in Auschwitz for mothers and daughters to be together. Most of the women who entered the camp after passing the selection were girls and women between the ages of sixteen and forty. Anna was forty-seven; her daughter, Ágnes, was twenty-one. Although more mothers and daughters were admitted into the camp together following the large influx of Hungarian Jews in 1944, Anna really passed the selection by chance, considering the fact she suffered from rheumatism. Both Anna and Ágnes were admitted to the Hungarian women's camp in Birkenau – the C lager. Once there, like others with family ties, they quickly learned to hide their relationship from camp officials in order to avoid separation and intentional abuse.

Mothers and daughters engaged in a constant, joint struggle for survival, characterized by the fierce desire to stay together. Anna and Ágnes's relationship was similar to other mother-daughter relationships in the camps: a shared survival struggle, constant pain as one watches the other's suffering, and the process of role reversal between mothers – who traditionally protect their daughters – and daughters, who tried to manage the survival struggle for both as their mothers got weaker. Anna describes the way her daughter tried to console her during the first days of their imprisonment in Auschwitz, and how these touching attempts gave her some solace, but also increased their mutual grief. She also relays how other daughters in the block were bitterly glad their mothers didn't have to suffer: "My dear little daughter snuggled up to me and this was such a sweet, reassuring feeling, but at the same time it was terrible to witness each other's suffering. She would soon be sobbing, seeing me on my knees for the first time. The other daughters kept consoling themselves: how fortunate that our mothers did not end up here; we could not bear to see them kneel down, and we would die if ever someone slapped them in the face."

Throughout, Anna and Ágnes try to protect each other physically and emotionally. When Ágnes lands better work, she manages to bring her mother extra food. After they are sent to the Schlesiersee camp, Anna does the same. When they are smuggled a farewell note from Anna's husband in the men's camp, they try to bear their personal anguish individually, so as not to burden each other. "Ági didn't say anything and neither did I. We kept looking at each other with encouraging smiles, even when our hearts were about to break."

Between the frequent selections and Anna's deteriorating health, Ágnes is constantly afraid of being separated from her mother. Anna describes her daughter's concern that she might be taken to death in one of the selections: "Ági didn't have a peaceful moment on account of me. It was her idée fixe that a selection would occur while she was working near the kitchen and we'd be separated." Luckily, both were transferred together out of Auschwitz. Following the collapse of the Eastern Front, a group of Jewish women was sent from Auschwitz-Birkenau to the border between Czechoslovakia and Germany where they worked in the Schlesiersee forced labour camp from October 1944 until January 1945.

The conditions in this small camp were horrible and female prisoners were assigned ruthless labour, digging anti-tank trenches in the cold and frozen ground. Anna writes that she actually preferred Auschwitz over this camp, as she feels herself breaking down. Yet, she tries to bear the hardship to protect Ágnes. "In spite of all my pains, I kept shovelling. By the evening, on our way back, I couldn't stand on my feet […] It was agony. I would have liked to scream, but I didn't want to aggrieve Ági further, so I suffered in silent desperation."

When Ágnes develops an infection in her leg due to the hard labour in the camp, she is forced to go to the camp hospital. Her condition doesn't improve and as the front moves closer and the camp prepares to evacuate and begin what became a "death march," Anna begs her to come with them rather than stay behind with the other patients. If she stays, Anna says, she will stay with her to suffer a similar fate: "[…] I went to see Ági and asked her to get up and try to walk. She got out of bed, but she could hardly make it over to the window. 'I would like you to come, my Ágika. It would be better for you to go with our friends than to stay behind with the sick,' I said. 'I can't, no matter how hard I try,' she answered despondently. I then raised my voice and spoke firmly to her, while my heart was breaking, 'My Ágika, you've got to come, your life is at stake.' She did. God performed a miracle – not for the first time, and not for the last time."

On the evening of January 21, 1945, the camp prisoners were evacuated from Schlesiersee. Following a ninety-five kilometre march on foot, they stopped for one night at the Grünberg camp. On January 29, 1945, about 1,350 women left Grünberg, divided into two groups. One was sent in the direction of Bergen-Belsen; the other, of which Anna and Ágnes were part, toward Christianstadt. The agonizing "death march" continued on a murderous journey that, for some, lasted 106 days, during which their fate was dependent on the perils of the journey and the mood of their guards, who killed anyone that stumbled or tried to escape. By May 4, 1945, only three hundred women had survived the eight hundred kilometre march to their destination, the town of Volary, Czechoslovakia. [6]

Throughout the first part of the march, as Anna gets weaker, Anna and Ágnes discuss escaping, as a few others have been able to do, but they are abruptly separated when Anna makes a fateful decision after leaving the Grünberg camp. "I was incapable of walking. 'My Ágika, let us flee!' I implored. But she didn't dare. Sensing that I was about to collapse, and dreading to be shot in front of Ági and having her fall behind because of me and suffer the same fate, I made my decision…. I was hoping that Ági was following me." Anna starts an independent, bitter, hard and lonely journey. She is traumatized, suffering from harsh guilt, throughout her wandering and hardship.

Upon liberation, Anna begins a journey back to their home in Szatmár. Her loneliness, a characteristic so evident in early testimonies and manuscripts, is ever-present and lingering. Not knowing what has become of her loved ones, she, like her old house, is full of emptiness and anticipation. "On Tuesday, April 3, at night, my train pulled into Szatmár. I clutched my heart because I felt it was going to jump out of my chest, whether from joy or sorrow, I couldn't tell. I was home, but alone. I had come back, but for what? By the time my loved ones – God willing – come back, a warm home will be waiting for them, where we will try to forget the horrors we endured and will try to heal each other's painful wounds."

The manuscript ends with the words of a woman who, despite all her loss, remained a person seeking a new and better world: "Only a new world built on equality can compensate for the inhuman suffering and martyrdom of hundreds of thousands and millions. And only

------

6   http://www.yadvashem.org/yv/en/exhibitions/death_march/artifacts/06.asp.

when we have accomplished this will our dear dead of holy remembrance – victims of human cruelty and madness – ever rest in peace in their graves."

Naʾama Shik
Yad Vashem International School for Holocaust Studies
2014

FURTHER READING

Baer, R. E., Goldenberg, M., eds., *Experience and Expression: Women, the Nazis, and the Holocaust*. Detroit: Wayne State University Press, 2003.

Bergen, D., ed., *Lessons & Legacies VIII:From Generation to Generation*. Evanston: Northwestern University Press, 2008.

Browning, C., *Remembering Survival: Inside a Nazi Slave-Labor Camp*. New York: W.W. Norton & Co., 2010.

Gutman, Y., Berenbaum, M., eds., *Anatomy of the Auschwitz Death Camp*. Bloomington: Indiana University Press, 1994.

Hertzog, D., ed., *Brutality and Desire: War and Sexuality in Europe's Twentieth Century*. New York: Palgrave Macmillan, 2009.

Ofer, D., and Weitzman, J. L., eds., *Women in the Holocaust*. New Haven and London: Vail-Ballou Press, 1998.

Mirom, G., ed., Shulhani, S., co-editor, *The Yad Vashem Encyclopedia of the Ghettos During the Holocaust*. Jerusalem: Yad Vashem, 2010.

Rozett, R., *Conscripted Slaves: Hungarian Jewish Forced Laborers on the Eastern Front During the Second World War*. Jerusalem: Yad Vashem, 2014.

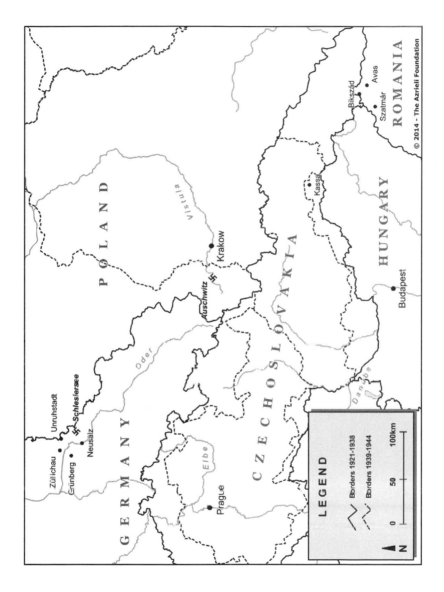

POLAND

GERMANY

Züllichau
Unruhstadt
Schlesiersee
Grünberg
Neusalz

Oder

Vistula

Krakow

Auschwitz

CZECHOSLOVAKIA

Elbe

Prague

Danube

Kassa

HUNGARY

Budapest

ROMANIA

Bikszád
Avas
Szatmár

© 2014 - The Azrieli Foundation

LEGEND

Borders 1921-1938
Borders 1939-1944

0   50   100km

N

In commemoration of our mother, Fanny (née Moskovits) Molnár, the widow of Henrik Molnár. She was killed in one of the gas chambers of Auschwitz at the age of eighty-four on June 3, 1944, and was incinerated in one of the many crematoriums. She will be mourned by those of us who stayed alive by the arbitrary mercy of fate.

To our dear, good mother, may this book be your gravestone. We are not able to erect a real one, made of marble, because you do not have a grave. Your tired body was not granted the chance to rest in the cemetery of Szatmár and your dust could not mingle with the dust of your beloved husband, Henrik, and daughter Margit. We, your children, were not given the chance to place a flower on your grave.

It was the wind of Auschwitz that scattered your dear ashes together with the ashes of many hundreds of thousands of other mothers, fathers, brothers and sisters, husbands, wives and children – to the eternal shame of those who brought about this catastrophe but also those who, whether with glee or pity, tolerated it.

Author's Preface

The pen is shaking in my paralyzed hand as I write: I AM ALIVE!

The only one who can fully feel what it means to live is someone who has been as close to death as I was, who has been touched by its icy breath, who, like me, was nearly buried. I am alive, and it is May again! The lilacs are in bloom and I smell their sweet fragrance again! There was springtime last year as well, but I didn't notice it. The lilacs were in bloom, but to me they seemed to be the black of mourning. They smelled sweet but I turned away from them because who could take pleasure in spring in a ghetto? In that sea of hatred, humiliations and tears, who could notice the lilac-hued glory of the bushes?

We had no eyes for beauty. Our noses could only perceive the stench of human cruelty, vileness, insanity. Our lips forgot how to smile; our hearts ached. And now I'm alive again! I can take delight in this new spring because I am still waiting, still hoping that my loved ones will return home. If they don't come home, if I wait in vain and I can no longer hope, then there will never be spring again and the lilacs will bloom only over my grave, over my shattered heart.

Szatmár, May 1, 1945

Occupation

On March 19, 1944, a bright spring morning in Budapest, I was awakened by the phone ringing in my room at the Gellért hotel and health spa, where I was undergoing treatment for my sciatica. I thought it would be my daughter, as she had come to Budapest a few days earlier to be with her fiancé, who was on furlough from the Labour Service.[1] Instead, it was my sister-in-law, Margitka, who I assumed was calling to ask about my well-being.

"I'm able to stand up," I said happily, "and I'm meeting a few of my girlfriends this afternoon. You should come, too."

"You mean to say that you don't know what has happened?" she asked, agitated.

"No, I haven't heard a thing," I answered, alarmed. "For God's sake, why are you so worked up?"

"Because the Germans occupied Hungary and Budapest this morning."

---

1 For information on the Labour Service, as well as on other historical, religious and cultural terms; major organizations; significant historical events and people; geographical locations; and foreign-language words and expressions contained in the text, please see the glossary.

"That's impossible!" I exclaimed. "Yesterday the city was still, completely calm. No one suspected a thing!"

"True, but today at dawn, the German army arrived in Budapest in hundreds of grey vehicles. Get dressed fast and go to the lobby, where they will surely have more information."

I slammed the receiver down. A cold fear gripped my heart and set it beating wildly. As I grabbed my clothes and quickly put them on, a picture appeared in my mind of the Christmas my husband, Zoltán, and I had spent in Zurich in 1938. On the way there, we had stopped for two days in Hitler's Vienna. By then, Vienna, where we used to spend many happy days and nights, was a mere shadow of the sparkling cosmopolitan city it had been. Jews from other countries were permitted to stay at the Grand Hotel Wien, which was designated an international hotel for foreigners. We stayed there, too, just as we had on other occasions. If the situation had not been so tragic, it would have seemed comical – bearded Jews were enjoying the excellent Viennese cuisine, quite unperturbed, alongside German officers.

When we visited my elderly aunt, she described the atrocities that the Viennese Jews had been enduring. She had witnessed people being thrown from fifth-floor apartments, people being tortured and killed. Hitler had declared his intention to inflict the same fate on the whole of European Jewry. My aunt practically begged us, on her knees, not to wait until Hitler's madness reached us as well. She was convinced that the same fate awaited us. Hitler, this wild beast set loose on Europe, would carry out his despicable plan and there would be no Jews left in Europe. She had already helped her children escape to England, but before she too could leave, her husband fell ill and died. She was left behind, penniless and desolate.

Zoltán and I had looked at one another, shocked. We said our tearful goodbyes to my aunt who, soon after our return home, wrote us that she was about to be transported to Lublin. In the letter, she urged us once more to save ourselves and escape, even if we had to leave everything behind. However, we did not take her advice; we couldn't believe that such horrible acts could go on in the twentieth century, nor that they could happen to us Hungarian Jews.

These memories flashed through my mind in seconds and I came to a frightening realization: we were wrong. The fate of the German Jews had caught up with us. We had waited too long, out of stupid optimism. I rushed down to the lobby and saw a lot of commotion, people milling about and a number of grey cars parked in front of the doors. Elegant German officers were conferring with the concierge, who later recounted that the Germans had demanded the hotel be evacuated. Professor Bilkei Papp, the director, had been outraged and adamantly refused. He told them to go and evacuate another hotel, as he wouldn't put his patients out on the street. They left, angry over not being able to procure the beautiful Hotel Gellért for their commanding officers, and immediately evacuated and occupied three other luxury hotels.

I sat in the hotel lobby, wondering what to do. I would have needed one more week to finish my treatment. Should I stay and calmly finish the treatment, or hurry back home to our family in Szatmár? As I debated what to do, I saw the pale and worried faces of those entering and exiting through the revolving door. People had just come to the realization of what had happened: Hungary had lost its independence! I didn't know whether the takeover had been hostile or friendly, but I did know that Hitler would turn the country into one of his lackeys that would blindly obey and serve his evil agenda.

The door revolved again and my daughter, Ágnes, a smile on her face, arrived with her fiancé, Pali Radváner. As befits young lovers, they were totally engrossed in one another; their beaming faces led me to suspect that they hadn't heard the news yet. They both turned pale when I told them what had happened. Ágnes's first reaction was that we should set out for home so as not to be separated from our loved ones, my husband, my son and my mother.

Pali had to return to his Labour Service company, so we decided that all three of us would depart the following morning. I wondered whether it might be wiser to stay on, whether the city would be a better place to endure all the changes and the turmoil that could ensue. I thought about calling our family at home and asking them to join us here to see how the situation would evolve, but the phone connections with the countryside were down.

Then my best friend from Szatmár, Mrs. Irma (née Reiter) Klein, came through the door. She was panicked, asking if we were planning to leave that night. "Out of the question," I replied. "Tonight there will be a huge crowd of people leaving from the hotels that have been evacuated, and we are better off going in the morning." It took a great deal of effort to talk her into waiting with us. The next morning, at the train station, we found out that the previous evening everyone had had to show their identity papers. The Jews were arrested, beaten up and interned. In other words, it was the beginning of the reign of terror. It had been a stroke of luck to wait.

Ági's farewell to Pali was emotional and, even then, I had a bad feeling about when and how those two would see each other again. Yet even in our worst nightmares, we couldn't have imagined the tragic circumstances under which they would next meet.

We set out on our trip with mixed feelings but arrived home without incident, to the great joy of our anxious family. In Szatmár everything was perfectly calm. With no sign of the Germans, we acknowledged that it had been a wise decision to come home after all, especially in light of the alarming stories continually relayed by Margitka in Budapest, who had first alerted me to the news of the German occupation. Girls were being picked up and dragged off to work detail, she said, and Jews were being insulted and attacked. We were in a constant state of anxiety over our family in Budapest.

However, by the end of March, the Germans were in Szatmár. Exhausted, dust-covered soldiers arrived on hundreds of white trucks that created an awful racket in the small city. Immediately after their retreat from the Soviet Union, they had travelled for three or four days without rest to reach Szatmár. Most of them were put up in the convent, to the concern of the nuns.

All you could hear in the city was the sound of cars. People were scared and living in silence, waiting to learn what tomorrow would bring. The first night, a Jewish oil manufacturer was shot to death. He had fought as an officer in Siberia during World War I. This had a devastating effect on the Jewish population. Fear set in, becoming our constant companion.

In addition to sensing our own impending tragedy, we also had to achingly acknowledge that Hungary was heading toward disaster. We were born as Hungarians and we were brought up as Hungarians. Hungary was our Mother. However, since September 6, 1940, when regent Miklós Horthy led the Hungarians to reclaim northern Transylvania, which included Szatmár, Jews had had to suffer one indignity after the other. By November 1940, Hungary had joined Germany as an Axis power and had progressively stripped us of our rights in an effort to prove that we were not Hungarian. We, who had given excellent writers, poets and artists to Hungary, and who had lovingly polished the Hungarian language as if it were a precious diamond, were looked down on as parasites by the "true" Hungarians. On the other hand, some Germans who had never mastered the Hungarian language, despite having lived very near to Budapest for centuries, were still viewed as "good" Hungarians. We had accepted all this with the dignity of the innocent, with our heads bowed, still hoping that better sense would prevail. We were foolishly waiting for our fate to be sealed, all the while counting on the much-touted Hungarian chivalry.

Passover neared and, as was our custom, we travelled the sixty kilometres to Bikszádfürdő, where my husband was the general manager of a lumber business and where we spent all of our vacations. One morning, we turned on the radio. This didn't happen often, since listening to the radio did not give us much pleasure anymore. All we heard was castigation of the Jewish people, to prepare public opinion for future actions. Now, ashen and silent, we listened to the government decree that obliged every Jew, or anyone deemed to be Jewish, to wear a yellow star.

This news had an especially devastating effect on my husband. I kept consoling him that everybody knew we were Jewish long before this and that it really didn't mean anything that from then on we'd be wearing a sign to that effect. But he could see beyond that. "This is the beginning of atrocities to come," he said. "This will be followed by decrees that will stipulate what those wearing yellow stars are 'not allowed' to do. A visible sign will unleash people's most despicable emotions and will subject those who wear it to the most brutal insults. This act has moved the Jews outside the protection of the law, and we will become free prey to our persecutors." Unfortunately, every one of his words and dire predictions soon became reality.

April 5, the day we had to put on the yellow star, arrived. In Bikszád, where Jewish citizens lived together in harmony with the Romanian and Hungarian population, we put on the star that we had only read about with disgust as an ancient, barbaric symbol that facilitated discrimination based on religion. However, we did not feel chastised. If we were treated with pity, we retorted that the only shame belonged to the ones who had come up with the regulation. We had no reason to feel ashamed. There were, of course, those who showed sympathy outwardly but rejoiced deep down; evil and simple-minded people always delighted in the fall of those they considered superior to them.

We kept hearing about people being attacked, beaten up, bullied and mobbed while wearing the yellow star. A few days later, my husband had to take the train back to Szatmár. Other travellers insulted Jews with yellow stars on the trains, so I was worried about him all day until his return. That evening, the children and I were waiting for him at the railway station. That morning, he had left as a gentleman, composed, but he returned as a broken, wan and dejected man. Fear pierced my heart, and I anxiously asked him if he had been assaulted on the train. He calmed me down, saying that this was not the case and he had made it home without a problem. However, I knew his every expression in the way that after twenty-three years of marriage one knows the man one loves and lives with, feels and suffers with.

I could tell that he had some bad news to deliver. I started quizzing him, wanting him to tell me what had happened, to share his troubles with me. I told him it would ease his heart, but he wouldn't say a word. We went to bed, but I could hear him tossing, turning, sighing. I implored him to tell me what had upset him so much. At last, he related to me that he had heard rumours that the Jewish population would be confined to a ghetto.

We spent the night worried, devising and rejecting a thousand escape plans. We feared for our daughter, Ágnes, especially, since she was a young woman – as well as in love and soon to be a bride – who could be subjected to the most terrible things. In my mind I could still see my husband's face, pale as death, after hearing some years ago about Slovak Jewish girls who had been rounded up, practically abducted, and transported to the front, where they fell prey to the soldiers. There is no point in writing about how we received this news as parents of a twenty-one-year-old daughter whom we had raised to lead a good, pure and virtuous life. The very thought of what was happening made us feel ill. Our first and foremost concern was how to save her from the atrocities. My seventeen-year-old son, János, was the pride of the whole family, yet we were preoccupied with our daughter's fate. After all, what could happen to a boy? At most, we thought, he would be taken away to do labour.

Ágnes, engaged since the previous Christmas to her long-time love, had been pleading with us to let them get married. I certainly wasn't against it, but my husband stuck to his old principled position that he would marry off his one and only cherished little girl when the war was over. He was the best, most devoted father; his only concerns were his family and his children's future, and in this matter he was adamant. He kept citing the example of our niece Zsófi, whose husband was taken to the Ukraine after only ten weeks of marriage. She had been living without him for two and a half years. Unable to settle anywhere, she travelled back and forth between her parents' house in Pest and her empty home in Szatmár, and she had a difficult time accepting her lot. He had a point there, but since the arrival of the Germans, I had been longing to go ahead with the wedding.

"Who knows what will happen next?" I said. "In the meantime, let them enjoy happiness." This argument settled the matter and Ágnes, thrilled, was allowed to write to Pali and ask him to procure the necessary papers for marriage. Pali replied in a telegram, "I will get the papers and take your daughter to my parents in Budapest." Had he arrived on time, they both would have escaped the subsequent horrors. However, it took a few weeks to obtain the papers, and meanwhile the tide of onrushing events carried us toward our destiny.

As the days passed, we constantly racked our brains to figure out a way to escape. One of the possibilities that emerged was to flee to the mountains and hide in the forest disguised in peasants' clothes. Our Romanian farmer friends were willing to take care of providing us with food, but I did not dare choose this solution. I knew that the authorities would be searching for us and that we would have to live the life of hunted game and be subject to the rigours of weather, with underground caves serving as our only shelter. I wouldn't be able to last through this, given my rheumatic legs. "How would you deal with a sick person with no doctor around?" I asked. "I would only become a burden and I might even jeopardize your escape." I was begging them to leave without me. My husband knew the woods very well and the children were young and strong and would probably survive the perilous life of partisans, but it was not for me. "I will manage on my own," I said. I thought that I might be able to flee to Romania and join my siblings there. Failing that, I could always take poison. I already had the poison in my possession; I'd gotten hold of it to be ready for all eventualities. Of course, I did not tell them about this.

My family would not hear of separation. Their motto was to stay together whatever happened, and this desire prevented us from carrying out any other plans. Thinking back, I don't understand why the idea of all four of us going to Romania never occurred to us. Most likely it seemed impractical at the time, even though a few thousand people had already managed to escape the hands of the hangman this way. I recently learned that some Romanian border guards actively helped Jews cross the border. We, however, were not aware of this then. We thought that people caught crossing the border illegally would be shot. After all, there were Germans all over Romania as well. Although many Romanians collaborated with the Nazi regime and only parts of Romania might have been safe for Jews, some Romanians knew better than to slavishly assist Hitler's henchmen in the execution of millions.

All along, Ágnes kept hoping that Pali would show up and that her own problem would be resolved in the best possible way. We were caring and anxious parents, and could see that Pali wasn't having any success in obtaining the necessary papers, so we kept coming up with viable and not-so-viable schemes as to how to help her escape and where to hide her. We thought we could get her false papers proving she was a gentile so she could go where no one knew her and find a job under a new identity. A village notary offered to give us the birth certificate of a girl born the same year as Ágnes who had passed away a long time ago. He would also include the papers of the parents and grandparents because the fact of having been born gentile was not alone sufficient: according to the defenders of "Christianity," a grandfather would be dragged from the grave to bear testimony to the purity of the grandchild's race. Unfortunately, the notary changed his mind at the last minute and asked to have the papers back. He worried he'd be found out, which would cost him his job, or worse. Having always been reasonable people, we returned the documents already in our possession.

A good friend of Ágnes's, Mária Finta, gave her a travel document that would allow her to go somewhere and take a job working with children. I warned this friend, a teacher, that this could lead to grave consequences for her. Nonetheless, shaking with sobs, she assured us that did not matter. She was fond of us, having spent months in our house as Ágnes's Romanian language instructor, and couldn't stand what was happening to us. She said that she didn't care if she got killed on our account.

My God, what consolation such devotion was. Realizing that there weren't only cruel beasts in our midst renewed our desire to live. We came up with a plan: Ágnes would go to Kolozsvár using Mária Finta's papers and work as a governess, possibly with a Romanian family. She spoke fluent Romanian, having finished her schooling in the language, and she loved children. The solution appeared ideal but when it came time to carry out the plan, Ági refused. She maintained that she didn't want to escape without us; come what may, at least we would be together. She was a gentle, sensitive girl who had never uttered an untrue word – how could she live a lie and betray people's trust, using someone else's name and assuming someone else's past? Today we know that thousands of young women escaped deportation and death this way, but at the time it seemed like such a terribly huge undertaking.

In mid-April, we spent our Easter holidays preoccupied with problems, worries and soul-searching, and then we had to travel back to Szatmár. Our hearts ached at leaving Bikszád, where we had spent the most wonderful ten years of our lives, where our children had grown up and where we knew and loved every stone and tree. We were somehow aware that this leave-taking was our last. We would never again see the gentle valley of Avas, the mountains that had witnessed our carefree ramblings and that surrounded this little enclave of simple, honest Romanian people. We couldn't find the words to express it, but our eyes and hearts said goodbye, forever, to the happy past.

On a Sunday morning, two announcements captured our attention in the newspaper. One read: Every Jew is obliged to present himself at his place of residence within twenty-four hours. The second: As of today, Jews are required to obtain a permit from the gendarmerie in order to travel. Since we were planning our trip for that very afternoon, my husband went to the gendarmerie to request permission. "It's true that the decree was passed," the sergeant said politely, "but we don't have the proper forms yet, so we cannot give you a permit for the journey. However, Mr. Director, since you need to present yourself in Szatmár, please, go ahead and make the trip with your family and I will take full responsibility for it." This eased our minds as the sad moment approached for us to board the train that would carry us toward the unknown, tearing us away from everything we held dear.

All the office staff of the lumber factory showed up at the station. Everyone was crying but our eyes were dry, our heads held high as we said our goodbyes, trying to conceal the bitter pain in our hearts with a smile. As we boarded, my son, János, a mere boy in Grade 11, turned to me and said, "Mum, please remember, we have just signed our death sentences." These words, this premonition, resonated often in my ears amidst the terrors of Auschwitz. He had spoken the truth. This journey marked the beginning of our true Calvary.

The train pulled out and we settled into our seats and sat quietly, lost in our thoughts. When we reached the first station, Avasfelsőfalu, a man in civilian clothes stormed onto the train, heading straight for us, and rudely demanded our travel permits. My husband reiterated what the sergeant had told him. "I'm not interested!" he screamed. "Get off the train immediately and take your luggage with you, you filthy Jewish lot."

My husband tried to explain our situation, but the plainclothes detective raised his fist menacingly, so we gathered up our belongings and disembarked. We were well known in Avas, so the Jews and Romanians assembled at the station were quite shocked to see us heading toward the village accompanied by a gendarme. Some people helped us with our luggage and followed us to the gendarmerie in a sort of caravan. We were kept waiting, of course, until the train had left, and that's when the detective called the sergeant in Bikszád. Since our story was substantiated, word for word, he had no choice but to let us go, screaming all the while that if there was ever a repeat of this incident, he'd show us who was boss. "Don't even think of escaping, don't dare get in a car," he shouted, "because I've got my eye on you!"

Whenever we drove through Avas, which was about once a week, we stopped at the pharmacy for a chat with our kind acquaintance, the pharmacist Ilonka Bernát. As is the custom in villages, the pharmacy doubled as the social club, the meeting place of the local intelligentsia. We headed there now because the next train wouldn't be leaving until nine in the evening, which meant a five- or six-hour wait in the village.

The local Jewish community was outraged as they listened to our story. The sight of my husband accompanied by a gendarme had had a terrible impact, given his position as one of the most influential people in Avas. That's when they realized how serious and bleak the situation was. If my husband, who was always ready to help others, couldn't even help his own family, what would become of them?

Ilonka served us a lovely afternoon snack in the pharmacy, and we enjoyed a pleasant conversation until it was time for the train to leave. By then someone had procured a car, our luggage was loaded on it and we drove to the railway station. Ilonka Bernát would later play an important role in shaping our destiny. I write her name as an expression of my eternal gratitude, and in the hope that one day she will return home and read my writing.

We arrived in Szatmár at two in the morning. On foot, we carried our many bags into the deserted city. Not a soul was in sight except for the German soldiers patrolling the streets, but they left us alone. We went to bed at last, weary, broken and exhausted, both physically and mentally.

Eviction

We were roused from our restless sleep by the strident ringing of the doorbell. Just as the maid, frightened, came in to announce that a policeman was looking for my husband, the policeman entered our bedroom. In a polite tone, he said, "Don't be alarmed, there is no problem, I would just like to ask Mr. Director to quickly get dressed, and Mrs. Hegedűs to pack two sets of underwear for him and enough food for two days." I asked him to leave the room while I got out of bed but he insisted that he could not, nor even turn his back. Most likely, he was supposed to keep an eye on us to make sure that my husband did not commit suicide.

We both got up with wild panic in our hearts, appearing calm on the surface. Zoltán started to get dressed and I began to pack as the policeman continued to reassure us that there wouldn't be any problem. My husband said goodbye to me, Ágnes and János, who were terrified, but we all held back our tears valiantly. We burst out crying only when he and the policeman had left the apartment. Dr. Endre Borgida, an elderly and ailing lawyer, was also taken from the building.

No sooner had they left than the doorbell rang again. Even in those early days, every ring of the doorbell jangled our nerves and made our hearts race, as we could not expect anything good from any new arrival. But what came next exceeded all our expectations. In burst a cocky, young Hungarian officer, whom I happened to know by sight. It was Lieutenant Solyom, a leader of Levente, the fascist youth corps. He was an infamous antisemite and sadist who habitually beat up and tortured not only Jews but even the gentile Levente members. He didn't bother to introduce himself. "I want to see the apartment," he declared at the top of his voice.

The army had already claimed two rooms of my apartment. One was occupied by a physician and ensign, a rather decent man who, after my husband was taken away, came to offer his assistance in case I needed anything. I concluded that the lieutenant was interested in the other room requisitioned by the army and I indicated exactly that. "I told you I am interested in the apartment, not this room!" he shouted vehemently.

Shocked, I asked, "Are you telling me that you want to take over the whole apartment?"

"No, that's not the case," he answered in an honest manner, just as one would expect of an officer. Then, he rushed out.

He reappeared an hour later with his wife, a farmer's daughter whom he had married along with her three hundred acres. This young woman in her twenties came in without saying hello, looked over the apartment, and, with her nose in the air, declared that it would do. That didn't surprise me – we had moved into this beautiful, brand-new place only three weeks earlier. She stated that I had to hand over the apartment in twenty-four hours and that I needed to vacate the premises right away. I thought I hadn't heard her right. "You might have the right to throw me out of this apartment in my own building," I said, "but I demand to have the order in writing. On second thought, I will not move out. I have no place to go. You may throw me out on the street if you feel you have the right." At that point, she declared that I could leave the furniture behind if there wasn't any place to store it, but the curtains and curtain rods belonged to the apartment, so I could not remove them. This was a novel assertion, but in those days bigger surprises were a regular occurrence.

I had had enough excitement for one morning, and left to find out what had happened to my husband and the others who had been picked up along with him. I met up with my girlfriends who were busy trying to deal with the same problem. In all, eighty prominent Jews had been arrested – doctors, lawyers, factory owners, wholesalers – in other words, anyone who was considered sufficiently wealthy.

We managed to get permission to provide dinner for the men and took turns cooking sumptuous meals at the community kitchen. Ági signed up as courier and carried the cauldron just to be able to see her adored father and talk to him. In this way, we found out that the men had not been harmed. A Gestapo officer was conducting an investigation into their financial affairs.

My mind somewhat eased about my husband, I dashed to the hospital to see my dear mother, who had been admitted with a case of pneumonia. She had fallen ill while we were in Bikszád. My sister Erzsike Blum, whom my mother lived with, had taken her to the hospital. She was out of danger as far as the pneumonia was concerned, and we were overjoyed to see one another. I told her about the pleasant time we had had in Bikszád and that we were all well and weren't having any problems. I said that the only reason Zoltán hadn't come to visit was that he had been called away on business. Our prime concern was to shelter her from anything that might trouble her, to spare her the disturbances that each new day brought. After all, it could cause her to take a fatal turn to learn that her son-in-law, whom she loved as if he were her own son, was in prison, that we had been ordered off the train, and that we were about to be evicted from our own home. Let her continue in blissful ignorance for as long as possible.

I anxiously awaited her full recovery and rejoiced to learn that she was over the crisis. If I'd had an inkling of what the future held in store for us, I would have begged God to take her soul then, to spare her the ghetto and the trauma of deportation at the age of eighty-four. Then we could have given her a burial, wept for her and mourned her, as was her due after having raised six children as a widow. Instead, once home from the hospital and restored to health, she found out all that had happened so far, and she would soon experience all that was to come.

The next day, I went downtown to find out whether Lieutenant Solyom had the right to throw me out of my apartment, and there I ran into a girlfriend of mine. "I guess," she said with a mournful face, "you haven't heard yet what happened." All the blood rushed out of my heart. Had something happened to my husband? Seeing my fear, she quickly continued, "The Germans ransacked your apartment." Relieved that it was nothing worse, I hurried home to be received by a sight similar to the destruction of Jerusalem by the Romans. The contents of the wardrobes were scattered all over the floor; the beds were upended in the middle of the room. Frantically, our maid recounted how a German officer had burst in with a white-bearded civilian interpreter. They had headed straight for the wardrobes, opened them, scrutinized their contents, taken some items and tossed the rest aside. She had no idea exactly what was gone because she had been sent out of the room. I went to the other wardrobe where we kept our files, documents and other valuables, which at the time we still thought important, and in the lock I spotted a key I didn't recognize. I turned the key and the wardrobe opened – nothing had been touched.

The maid was surprised, since the intruders had not noticed the key and had sent her for a hatchet to break open the wardrobe. Instead, she had run to fetch the ensign, who wouldn't allow them to break open that beautiful piece of furniture. The ensign recounted the rest of the story: The Germans declared that they would seal the apartment, which was now officially requisitioned, and no one was allowed to enter it. The ensign protested, at which point they considered leaving his room open, but they did not accept this proposal until finally he pledged to ensure that we not remove anything from the apartment. The Germans left, carrying off quite a few items and promising to return soon to transport the rest away. In the meantime, no one was to touch a thing.

I stood, panic-stricken, slowly discovering how much was missing. First and foremost, the knapsack filled with all the essentials that I had prepared for my husband. How would I replace it? Among the missing items were pillows, duvets, men's underwear, János's suitcase that had not yet been unpacked since our return from Bikszád, and a lot of women's hosiery; there was not a handkerchief or stocking left in the whole house.

"What am I supposed to do?" I asked the physician. "The Hungarian officer ordered me to vacate the premises in one day. According to the German officer, I'm not allowed to remove anything. Where will this all lead? Whose orders should I follow?" He reassured me that I should just go ahead and tidy up the apartment. He was convinced that this attempt at thievery was a private undertaking on the part of the German officer en route from the front, and that we wouldn't ever see him again. He said that if I was still worried, I could store our valuables in his room.

Distressed, I ran upstairs to see my friend, whose elderly, ailing husband had been taken away along with mine. She was sitting, dejected, in her looted apartment. I found out from her that the man who had visited us was not an officer in transit but rather a lieutenant of the Gestapo, the same one who was in charge of guarding and interrogating our husbands. She had gleaned this from their conversation.

Later, while in the city, I learned that we had gotten off lightly compared to some, whose apartments were completely sealed, never to be entered again, not even to remove so much as a handkerchief. From then on, I didn't have a peaceful moment in the apartment, as there was always the chance that they would come back at any minute. I was worried day and night, and my only desire was to get away from this place.

Lieutenant Solyom soon showed up with the authorization to requisition the apartment and offered again, now in a congenial tone, to let me leave my furniture behind if I had no means to store it. I was not ready to do him this favour, but since I had no use for the light fixtures, I offered to leave them behind, at which point his wife interjected haughtily that she had no use for Jewish light fixtures. Amazingly, she didn't hold it against the curtains that they were Jewish! They kept those for good.

It was time to move, but where? I turned to the gentile manager of our factory for advice. He listened to my story with indignation and immediately offered to hand over his own apartment to us. "How could I accept such a sacrifice?" I asked.

"Just go ahead and move in without a second thought," he replied. It was rumoured that this part of the city would become the ghetto, in which case he'd have to move anyway. That's when the possibility really struck me for the first time, even though it had been mentioned frequently of late, that we would be returning to the Middle Ages, with Jews forced into ghettos.

I thought through his offer carefully but realized there was no point in accepting it. It made no sense to furnish a big apartment since, if this area did become the ghetto, I wouldn't be allowed to keep it anyway. I thanked our good and faithful friend for his kindness, and rented a large room on a street that was sure to be included in the ghetto. I furnished it handsomely and thus freed myself from the chore of taking care of a large apartment and household, for which I no longer had any patience. I had much greater problems to deal with.

Among all my concerns, the one that weighed most heavily on my mind was still Ágnes. How could I save her from the ghetto? Where could I hide her before moving there with my son? I didn't want her to accompany us, as I was tormented day and night by horrible images. It would simply drive you mad, just imagining what might happen to young women exposed to every whim of the German soldiers.

During those days of tribulations, a kind Christian friend of ours, Gizi (née Strempl) Steier, was a true support. She and I discussed what needed to be done and, with my husband under arrest, it was she who took care of our affairs. She stood by us body and soul. She suggested that we send Ágnes to a convent in Felsőbánya, where she had good connections as her son had been schooled there for several years. She could take Ágnes and enroll her as a student. Ágnes was willing to entertain the idea. She had always done her studies at a convent and she liked the sisters; her only concern was how she would be able to correspond with her fiancé from there, but we set that aside for the time being. We packed her oldest outfits, the ones from her school days: black stockings, shoes, cotton underwear left over from my trousseau, all the while laughing at the prospect of how this fashionable young lady would look in such garb. We agreed that Gizi would pick her up in a car the next morning, and since those wearing a yellow star were not able to travel anymore, Gizi would also procure some gentile identity documents for her.

After having made the big decision, Ágnes spent the whole night crying at the thought, once again, of being separated from us, and when Gizi arrived the next morning, Ági implored us not to subject her – perhaps needlessly – to the anxieties of travelling with false papers. Let Gizi travel alone, she said, and once it was certain that she had been accepted, she would go back with her the following day. In vain, Gizi tried to cajole her into sticking with the original plan, in case some obstacle might arise, but she could not convince Ági to accompany her. Gizi drove off alone and returned that same evening, beaming. "It's all arranged," she said. "It's a pity though, that Ágnes did not come along, because she could have moved in right away."

The head of the convent school had driven back with Gizi to discuss the financial arrangements and to take Ági back with her the next day. In the meantime, Ági had come to accept this solution, and while we were trying to figure out how she could manage to keep corresponding with Pali, a letter arrived from the mother superior. She wrote that they would not authorize Ágnes's enrolment, that they were afraid of the consequences. Our joy exceeded our disappointment: Fate wanted us to stay together after all! We had passed up the last chance for her escape.

The next day, May 3, the ghetto order was issued. I started dashing around to place my furniture and other valuables with gentile acquaintances and friends, so that I would be ready to move as soon as possible. When all was done and my lovely new apartment that I had outfitted only a few weeks earlier stood empty, I said goodbye to the physician-ensign who had shared our trials during these awful days. "You see," I said to the doctor, "this is what it looks like when they put into practice those things that sound so 'appealing' in the editorials: *Let's break the spirit of the Jews; let's bring them to their ruin.* Here, a happy home has fallen apart; a happy family, whose only thought was for each other, has become destitute and homeless."

I moved into the ghetto well ahead of time and was next faced with the problem regarding the "Declaration of Property." I had to do this all on my own and in the most detailed fashion possible, including each and every asset, all the while being threatened with what would be done to those who made a false declaration or left something out. The spectre of internment was constantly thrust in our faces and, in our naivety, we never imagined what a delight internment might have been compared to what actually awaited us. Thus, I declared every valuable without a single omission, and listed the names of our gentile friends who were storing my surplus furniture and items of value.

At the same time, my husband, imprisoned, was also being interrogated on the same subject. I was fearful of inadvertently contradicting him. Indeed, I was living in fear of everything. After dealing with this matter, I could at last go out to see my mother, who had been brought home from the hospital. I also needed to do some grocery shopping, which I hadn't been able to find time for amidst all of my problems. Needless to say, we had to stock up on goods for our life in the ghetto.

My errands complete, I headed to my new home, the ghetto. On the way, a troop of soldiers drew up beside me and broke into a horrible Jew-baiting song, full of the most obscene insults. It made my face burn. I started running like someone being pursued, and it wasn't until I arrived home that I finally glanced at the newspaper I had picked up earlier. This was the antisemitic rag called *Szamos*, run by Mr. Albert Figus, a former freemason and a current member of parliament for the Arrow Cross Party.

The announcement right on the front page, in large type, read: "The gates to the ghetto will be closed as of four o'clock this afternoon and no one will be allowed to leave through them. Starting tomorrow, Jews will be forced to move into the ghetto from the city." The signatories, county prefect Barnabás Endrődi and Mayor Lászlo Csóka, had proudly completed their work for László Endre, the antisemitic hangman-in-chief who organized the establishment of the ghettos. Perhaps he would recommend these glorious patriots for higher honours.

The Ghetto

I had known that the ghetto order was coming and had dreaded it, but how I felt when the gates closed behind me is difficult to describe. There is no word to express the heartache of being wronged in one's human dignity, the emotions of innocent people condemned. I was a prisoner, even if it wasn't within four walls. I was a captive without any hope of escape.

The next day, in the pouring rain, the transport of Jews to the ghetto began. The first ones arrived from the surrounding villages, broken and wretched men, women and children with bundles on their backs. Their faces were full of fear, their eyes full of pain. The next group came from the city, block by block, evacuated by a committee of civilians and policemen who had allowed them to bring only a few items – clothing, underwear, bed linens and food – no money or other valuables. The wealthier Jewish families loaded the remainder of their lives and possessions onto carts and trudged behind them with bundles on their backs. The poorer Jews did not have to move – they had already been living in that part of the city where the ghetto was formed.

A jeering crowd lined the streets. Only behind a few windows could one see eyes wet with tears, but even these tender-hearted souls, ashamed, tried to hide their sympathy by withdrawing quickly from the window, because the henchmen who were lurking about considered it a crime to express any pity for us.

Once on the territory of the ghetto, the crowd was herded into the synagogue where the females – from young girls of ten to the eldest – were examined by midwives in case they had some valuables concealed in their bodies. Whose diabolical idea was this? Whose degenerate mind came up with it? Is this what my poor, kind, highly-esteemed, grey-haired mother had lived to the age of eighty-four to endure? She arrived beaten down and dispirited, together with my sister Erzsike, her husband, Dr. Ede Blum, and her stepson, Lali. Only then did I realize that I had been lucky to escape this indignity by moving into the ghetto in advance.

Over the following days, more and more new groups continued to arrive. It was so crowded you could hardly breathe. There was not even a handful of space left in the apartments, the furniture removed in order to accommodate all the people. Then, the occupants of the Nagykároly ghetto were brought in as well, among them many of our friends and relatives.

The newly formed Jewish council was tasked with assigning a place to each person and resolving any problems. However, the crème de la crème of Jewish society was then in police custody, and thus the council members were not necessarily those best suited to the task. Their president was a good choice, but he was a very old man, and the younger ones were more preoccupied with their own affairs than with those of the community.

The members of the council, together with their families, resided in the ghetto with the rest of the Jewish population. A few Jewish doctors who had been assigned to air-raid duty were the only ones still living in the city. They were our link with the outside world. One day, they arrived with the news that they would be staying in the city for good, apparently able to live in an apartment building designated with a yellow star. A few weeks later, they moved in all of their belongings, but when they themselves tried to move into the building, the doors were shut and they were loaded onto a truck and transported to the ghetto.

Each building in the ghetto resembled a busy beehive. There were about 17,000 people packed into three city blocks. The rooms were lined with mattresses pushed so tightly against each other that there was no space left to pass between them. We had to step on the mattresses to get across the room, sometimes trampling on people's feet. Even the smallest rooms had at least ten people living in them. Thirty of us, all relatives and good friends, occupied three rooms in a building owned by an old friend. We pooled our provisions and shared a common kitchen, posting a rota on the door of the various chores – cooking, cleaning, washing up – to be carried out by the women.

This same apartment building housed the families of some clerks and factory workers from Bikszád, and we found out that their sufferings had been even greater than ours. They had been detained for days, locked up in the synagogue without food or water. Anyone who tried to bring them food was prevented from going near the place. Then, bringing only as much as they could carry, they were forced to march along the road for fifty or so kilometres, stumbling under the physical and emotional weight of their loads.

Water in the ghetto was piped in from the city and a factory building was fitted up to be a hospital, and this somehow gave the appearance of permanence to our stay. We were among our own kind and this made ghetto life bearable. We didn't have to see the jeering faces, the despising smiles; we didn't have to hear the Jew-baiting songs of the soldiers and Leventes. Nobody talked about deportation. We figured we would live in the ghetto until the long-awaited miracle – the Red Star – would redeem us from the yellow star. But we waited in vain.

The young people were assigned different communal service roles: Ágnes became a nurse and János became a policeman, which greatly appealed to him and made him feel like a very important person. Each day, Ági eagerly awaited the arrival of her fiancé, vacillating between joy and concern. Mr. Sárközi, the ghetto commandant, a bow-legged, sideburn-sporting, gnome-like terror, promised, with a show of good humour, that he would not pose any obstacles to the marriage, and that as soon as Pali arrived, the pair could depart immediately. My husband, still in the jail, was handed the paternal consent form for his signature. Everything was in place – only the fiancé was missing.

Then the authorities began searching the houses of those who had already been living in the area prior to its becoming the ghetto. I was informed that as long as I surrendered all my valuables, no harm would befall me, but if they found anything that had not been declared and handed over, they would intern me. This menace of internment was like a popular refrain being played over and over. They even took our wedding bands; we had been allowed to retain them up to that point, but now they changed their minds. Amidst sobs, Ági removed her recently acquired precious treasure from her finger. "We have nothing of value any more," I said dejectedly. As soon as I picked up my fountain pen to sign the declaration, the head of the search committee pounced on me. "The pen has a gold tip and you failed to declare it. This is cause for internment!" Ultimately, he was satisfied with simply pocketing my beautiful pen, my cherished keepsake.

The same thing happened to the special little watch pinned to my dress. It was a fine, Swiss-made timepiece, inside a glass globe, and since it was not made of either silver or gold, I was not obliged to hand it over. However, this piece was also to the liking of this man, who quickly relieved me of the burden of it. "I will not proceed with the internment just this once," he said jovially, "but if we find anything else, there will be no getting out of it." After they left, I frantically went through every drawer in the house to check if there were any valuables hidden inside, but they never came back for another house search.

～

At last, after all the trouble, misfortune and suffering, there was something to rejoice about – my husband and his fellow prisoners were released! After almost four weeks of imprisonment, my beloved husband arrived all skinny and pale, but he came alive again as soon as he was in our midst. Now that the ghetto was in place, there was no need to keep anyone in jail. To our great surprise, even those who had been given life sentences were transported from the prison to the ghetto. We concluded that, in the authorities' estimation, the ghetto was worse than jail.

A few days later, a kid came running to us, announcing that the fiancé of Miss Ágnes was in front of the gate and was not being allowed to enter. Ágnes, not suspecting what a fatal step this would mean for the future, hurried to the gate all flushed with happiness and requested an entrance permit for him, as had been promised. It was graciously granted – most likely they were having a good laugh at our expense all the while – and Pali entered the ghetto. Oh, how fortunate he would have been had he not entered. Of course, the young couple only had eyes for each other. They arrived hand in hand, totally oblivious to the tragic circumstances under which they had been reunited. Our hearts grew even heavier. This was not how we had imagined the wedding of our one and only adored daughter. Oh, how we had been planning, how we had been preparing, for this most important step in the lifetime of a young woman. We had been saving up for her trousseau ever since she had reached the age of fifteen. There was a little nest being built for them in Buda, where they were to begin their happy married life. At that moment, all those desires, hopes and plans seemed to crumble.

We sent a telegram to Pali's kind-hearted old parents, confirming his safe arrival in Szatmár. They responded with a telegram of their own that expressed their good wishes, but it was a terrible blow to them to not be able to take part in the wedding of their most cherished son. They had previously sent his wedding outfit, but Ági had only one of her old suits in the ghetto, and therefore Pali felt it was more appropriate for him to wear his Labour Service clothing for the occasion.

The wedding took place on Saturday, May 13, at noon. They left

the ghetto accompanied by a policeman and a witness, our friend
Endre (Bandi) Wohl, whose house we were living in, and arrived at
city hall. Their second witness, Dr. Gusztáv Roóz, a childhood play-
mate of mine, was still living in the city because he was serving as an
air-raid doctor. He joined them at city hall.

I know, as I write this, that both of those witnesses are no longer
alive. A few days later, when, as I previously mentioned, Dr. Gusztáv
Roóz was supposed to be transferred to the ghetto along with all the
other physicians who were still living in the city at that point, he gave
poison to his wife and his mother and took some himself. He was
the only one who died at that time. His eighty-year-old mother and
his wife, an ophthalmologist, ended up in Auschwitz. I only recently
found out, while writing this memoir, that close to the end of the war,
Dr. Endre Wohl died of starvation.

Ágnes and Pali, the two sweetest, most gentle people in the world,
stood blissfully before the justice of the peace exchanging wedding
vows, having forgotten all the bitter trials of the past. There was no religious ceremony, and the "wedding feast" consisted of canned chick-
en soup. Their plan was to travel to Budapest and leave Ági with Pali's
parents, who were very fond of her. There was no talk of a ghetto in
Budapest yet, so we thought it a better idea for Ági to stay there, but
until their departure, what space could be found for the newlyweds in
a crowded building with ten people in each and every room?

One of Ági's friends, Kati (née Kalocsay) Havas, offered to hand
over her small kitchen, which currently provided shelter for herself,
her husband and her angelic little son, who was only a few months
old. They would move into the rooming house that their house had
been converted into in recent weeks. The young couple gladly accepted the invitation. So, with an aching heart but wearing a smile, I
set about to furnish and decorate the little chamber with white lilacs.
Let those flowers adorn their plain, unadorned nuptials. To think that
my daughter had been dreaming of a white wedding dress, a wreath
of myrtle, in a sanctuary decorated with lilacs, and this was what it

all amounted to: brief wedding vows and a police guard. The wedding may have lacked external trappings, but that was amply made up for by internal feelings of happiness and, most importantly, their immense love for each other and their optimism for better times to come. They were interested in only one thing: to be joined together at last after their long engagement, and they left on their honeymoon to the neighbour's place.

Feeling glum, I packed their suitcases for their trip to Budapest. The next day, all ready to go, they asked Mr. Sárközi for their travel permit. This tyrant laughed in their faces and declared, "One can only enter the ghetto; one cannot leave it." Instead of saving our daughter, even sweet Pali had to share the misfortune that had become our lot.

It was a few days later that the news reached us that the physicians living in the city would be brought to the ghetto. In addition to Dr. Gusztáv Roóz, Dr. Samu Fekete, a famous old ophthalmologist, and my husband's dearest friend, Dr. Oszkár György, an excellent radiologist, also attempted suicide. This news had a devastating effect on us. We grieved for them and at the same time we envied them, for having enough will to die but not enough to live. Dr. Oszkár György had also given poison to his mother, who had terminal cancer. At first he was resuscitated, and then his mother also had to be revived so that he would not be charged with murder. She was successfully revived, but in an unguarded moment, he strangled himself with the cord of his pyjamas. Thus ended the life of a young, vital and fine human being and physician. His mother died in the ghetto, released from her suffering.

A few days later, another horrible story raced through the ghetto like wildfire: A beautiful young girl, Annuska, the daughter of well respected journalist Sándor Dénes, had poisoned herself. Her gentile fiancé, an army officer, raged at the ghetto gates until Annuska's corpse was handed over to him. He buried her in her wedding dress, late at night, to avoid being an object of pity. Not even a Gothic novel, the product of a crazed imagination, could have depicted horrors of this kind.

Dr. Jenő Farkas, Szatmár's best lawyer, the wise optimist who shared our quarters in the ghetto, suffered a heart attack on hearing all this news. He was lying motionless for days. We took care not to excite him in any way. The already saddened house was now engulfed in the stifled silence that surrounds the gravely ill. His devoted wife managed to care for and rejuvenate him, only to later deliver him alive to the gas chambers of Auschwitz.

One of the buildings in the ghetto, 7 Báthory Street, had become infamous because it was turned into a torture chamber where the gendarme-bandits from Kolozsvár were using medieval methods. All those who, according to them, did not make a full declaration of their valuables, or hid them with gentile friends, were brought there. People staggered out of this house more dead than alive, bloody and beaten to a pulp. In the better case, they left on their own two feet, but most of the time they were carried out on a stretcher.

The numbed silence of the ghetto was pierced by ghastly death cries. Day and night, people worried it would be their turn, hearts racing, nerves strained, turning pale each time a door opened or a doorbell rang. Some of our housemates had already been taken away, among them my niece and her husband. We anxiously awaited their return. Their daughter, Kató, had been waiting for them on the street and suddenly she rushed in, distraught, saying, "They are coming, they can barely walk!" The poor souls arrived, staggering but forcing themselves to smile. The gendarmes had shown her some mercy – it was only her hands that bore the bloody welts inflicted by truncheons, but he had been beaten on the soles of his feet until he fainted from the excruciating pain. His whole body was covered in bruises but he did not confess, lest he put his gentile friends in harm's way.

My husband was also summoned, but he – and for this I will be forever grateful – concealed it from me and let me know where he had been only after his return. However, since I had declared everything properly and listed the names of our friends with whom we had left belongings for safekeeping, he was not harmed, and I was not cited.

The factory owner Sándor Gerő was beaten half to death, and when he dragged himself home, he took poison. Some of the women, among them the wife of Mr. Farkas, an engineer, were tortured to the point that they had to be taken directly to the hospital, and from there they were loaded on the hospital train bound for Auschwitz. A woman who lived in a building that faced ours went mad. There was no place to take her, and so we had to listen to her appalling and incoherent raving, which woke us at dawn and prevented us from falling asleep at night.

We were in a constant state of anxiety, and ghetto life was so unbearable that we were scarcely shocked when the authorities dropped a bombshell: we were going to be deported. Of course, we were under the impression that we would be sent to work, and we would gladly work as long as we could live in peace somewhere, together with our family, no matter how modest the circumstances. Two versions of where they were taking us circulated. According to one, we'd be transferred to work on the *puszta*, the plains, near Debrecen, and according to the other, a workers' settlement near Kassa. There was no talk at all of being transported out of the country; on the contrary, the minister responsible gave his word of honour to the Jewish council of Pest that this would not happen. Still, there were a few wise people, mostly among the religious Jews, who, at the news of deportation, managed to flee the ghetto with the help of the police or sometimes the German military, for a lot of money.

On May 18, the tenants of the first street were ordered to get ready. They were allowed to bring along two sets of underwear, two sets of clothes and some food. A lot of people volunteered to be on the first transport, out of fear of the torture chambers operating in the ghetto. We had thought that we would remain in the ghetto, so we had been very careful with our provisions. We knew that we couldn't count on getting a new supply. Although there had been a few days when good friends were allowed to bring parcels to the police guarding the ghetto, we hardly received any of what they brought; the police and the gendarmes consumed most of it. However, now that we knew we were to be taken away, we began to squander our provisions. We shared our food with those who did not have enough to last them for the duration of our stay. We kept eating and drinking to ensure that very little food would be left for the enjoyment of our oppressors. We also distributed our surplus clothes and underwear.

On May 19, the evacuation of the ghetto began. People were herded to the square, where they were stripped naked and once again subjected to an awful search, in case they had hidden something in their bodies. Their parcels were scattered and rifled through, a lot of the contents removed. Afterwards, the sad procession started off toward the railway station. Bundles on their backs, people clutched their children, who had been sentenced to death.

Never have I seen a more heart-wrenching sight.

Within about two weeks, the whole ghetto was emptied except for our street, which was scheduled to leave with the last transport. By this time, our nerves were so frayed from having witnessed the torment of tens of thousands of people, from having learned of the suicides of many friends, from endlessly agonizing over the dilemma of whether we should kill ourselves or be dragged into the unknown. We had all become wrecks.

My mother was constantly imploring my brother-in-law, a physician, to give her an injection of morphine to relieve her for good from the suffering that awaited her. She, who had always been known for her wisdom and intelligence, asked, "Why do I need to go through all this? I would like to rest beside my husband and daughter in our cemetery plot in Szatmár. Why do you let me be taken somewhere else to die? There is no way I will survive the adversities of the trip." I wish my brother-in-law had obliged and we had been able to bury her here. What solace it would give if she had not had to endure the distress of the trip, if the sighs of our grieving souls were able to fly over her grave rather than over the forever cursed fields of Auschwitz.

After such awful, panic-ridden days, the sorrowful day of the last transport arrived. On May 31, 1944, we were herded to the ghetto square. Our lives were all that counted and I was interested only in the fate of our family. I didn't give a thought to all that we had to leave behind: our new house, the result of thirty years of my husband's hard work, and all that we had managed to acquire and save up during our twenty-three years of marriage. I didn't care about any of it. As long as we were allowed to stay alive and together, nothing else mattered. Some of our housemates cried over each of their possessions. Our landlady said a tearful goodbye to every shrub in her garden, and she was already at the front door when she ran back to hide a nice new pot in the attic. The pot is probably still there, but she will never come home. She ended up in the crematorium.

At the square, we were put through the terrible search procedure and then sat on our bundles, dejected, waiting for the transfer. At the front door, we had parted with my mother, who as a favour had been accommodated on the hospital train to make her trip more comfortable, along with my sister Erzsike, who would ride in the physicians' car. We didn't say our goodbyes because we thought we would meet again once we arrived at our destination.

We were close to fainting from the terrible heat and were anxious to depart when – half an hour before the departure – my niece Zsófi's husband arrived at the ghetto, after serving two and a half years in the Ukraine. He entered of his own free will, having run away from his company to be with his wife and father. He had read cards postmarked "Waldsee" that the Germans forced deportees from Lower Carpathia to write on their arrival at Auschwitz, cards that read, "We are fine, the whole family is together, we are working, the food and our treatment are satisfactory." Of course, the purpose of making people write these cards was to ensure that Jews would not flee before deportation. Thus, the family was complete, and so was the tragedy. Both Ágnes's and Zsófi's young husbands came with us into our exile.

The procession began to move off. We loaded our parcels onto a small cart. My husband and the other men pushed it to the station, constantly wiping away the sweat running down their faces. Among the men was our landlord, Endre Wohl, a first lieutenant in the reserve army who had fought through four years of World War i and had pinned his medals onto his jacket to show the world how someone who had fought valiantly for the Hungarian homeland was being rewarded. Behind the cart, my son-in-law was pushing a dilapidated pram loaded with belongings that did not fit on the cart. Ági and I walked behind them with knapsacks, each carrying a roll of bed linen and small bags. Stooped under the weight of the parcels and the heartache, we made our way to the train station, through streets lined with curious onlookers.

It's impossible to ever forget the anguish of this passage. We relived our whole lives on this miserable road, just as a dying man supposedly does in his last moments. We said goodbye to the city where we had been born and brought up, had started a family, and had been very, very happy.

Our loved ones, even our great-grandparents, were resting here in the cemeteries, yet we were told this was not our homeland. I envied the dead as we passed by the cemetery. How much easier it was for them to lie among flowers, unaware of all that we were going through as we walked toward a horrible, uncertain future, knees buckled, degraded, defiled, carrying the achievements of a whole lifetime in our knapsacks.

Finally this Calvary ended as well, and we arrived at the station. Our plan was for the occupants of the Wohl building, about seventy people in all, to travel together in one cattle car. Perhaps it would be easier to bear our suffering among friends and relatives, and so we were waiting for the others, sitting glumly on our parcels. No sooner had we sat down than an officer of the gendarmerie, all spit and polish, stomped over and rudely yelled at us, ordering us to get into a cattle car that was missing exactly five people. We said that we were waiting for the other members of our family, but the officer took a swing at my husband, at which point we hurried like crazy to climb into the car, which already had seventy people jammed into it. Understandably, we were received with much grumbling, and we could hardly find any room to put down our parcels and sit on them.

As soon as we got in, the car was locked up.

Exile

We were prisoners of a by now inevitable destiny. Mentally and physically exhausted, I was sitting between my husband and my son, clasping the hands of each for reassurance. Ági and Pali were squeezed together on top of a suitcase. Their eyes revealed their despair, no matter how hard they tried to conceal it with a smile. This was not the way the poor dears had imagined their honeymoon.

Early afternoon had turned into late evening by the time everyone was loaded onto the cattle cars and the train departed for a dark and unknown destination. Were we really going to remain in the country? Were they taking us to Poland, which we knew meant certain death? These questions pressed upon our hearts. At one point, instead of fearing death, I longed for it, to save us from this gruesome journey. It felt like nothing could have been more horrible than this. Try to imagine seventy five people crammed into a locked-up car, where the only source of air and light were two tiny windows at either end of the car. In these crowded conditions, with total lack of privacy, we had to eat, sleep and perform our bodily functions. The buckets stank, and once they were full, their contents were disposed of through the windows.

As the miserable day and the even more miserable night passed, the mood grew increasingly tense and anxious. People wailed and screamed endlessly. Some held huge onions that reeked to high heavens. (What we would have given later on in Auschwitz for these despised onions!) People were cooking on kerosene stoves and others were changing diapers, neither of which did much to sweeten the pungent air. Mothers were nursing their babies, and fathers, in their heightened nervous states, were slapping the older kids around, airing the dirty linen of their lives before our eyes.

We sat half suspended, propping each other up, dozing off due to weariness and exhaustion but waking up with a start at every jolt, every few minutes. Furthermore, the intense heat of the day was replaced by heavy rain, which could have been a boon for us if the top of our car had not been so full of cracks. As it was, however, the rain beat down on us incessantly. All our possessions – blankets, clothes, bread – got soaked.

We kept changing our clothes, yet the rainwater was dripping down our skin under our garments. Eventually, we took all we owned out of our bags, but since there was no way to dry anything out, our clothes remained wet right through. We were completely drenched on the outside and yet we were parched for a drink of water. It was only after we begged and pleaded with people at the station that someone was willing to hand us some water through the window, and not for free. We gave them whatever we could in exchange: gloves, change purses, pocket knives. We handed over everything we had, just to slake the thirst of our parched lips. Soon enough there was nothing left to give, and so we no longer had water.

On June 1, we arrived at Kassa and the doors of our car were opened. We grew hopeful that we would be getting off and staying in the country. Instead, the same gendarme-hangman who had herded us into the car so rudely in Szatmár jumped aboard and read from a sheet of paper at the top of his voice that everyone was required to surrender everything made of leather, like change purses, wallets and gloves, in addition to knives and scissors, but most of all, money. There was to be a body search and if anyone had concealed something, they would be shot to death. He gave the leader of our group half an hour to collect these items and, locking the car door behind him, he moved on to intimidate the passengers of the next car. During that half hour, as everyone was collecting their few remaining trifles, a German officer sprang onboard declaring that if we dared to surrender any valuables to the Hungarians, we'd be shot. Our choice: die at the hands of our Hungarian "brother" or those of our enemy, the German soldier? We chose the middle road. We gave something to each of them, except this left us with nothing, not even a pocket knife to cut a bitter mouthful from our soggy bread.

All of a sudden the train started moving, ending our hopes that we would not be taken out of the country. Our worries were now compounded with the certain knowledge of our death sentence. After all, we had heard enough about Lublin and Dachau, the graveyard of millions. The unfamiliar names of Polish stations followed one after the other. My son, the little geography expert, was trying to figure out our route from these place names, but without a map it was difficult, and so we had no idea where we were. The train passed through spectacularly beautiful countryside, amidst high mountains that under different circumstances would have interested us but as things stood, it only increased our bitterness to see that green meadows, blue skies, gentle hills and majestic mountains still existed in the world while we were passing by them, half fainting from the heavy air laden with human stench.

On the morning of the second day, at last, the sign on the station bore a familiar name, Krakow. Finally we knew where we were. Soon after, when our train stopped at the station of Katowice, the railwayman informed us through the window that by the evening we would reach our destination: Auschwitz. We had never heard of this place before, so we were relieved when he said that we would be working there and that no harm would befall us.

We travelled on, and our train stopped in Auschwitz at dusk. We pushed and shoved each other to get to the window, curious to see where we had been brought. We could see something of a street, straight as an arrow, lined with barrack-like buildings on both sides. I was glad to see the power lines along the road, an indication that we wouldn't have to work at some kind of uncivilized location.

We had arrived but the car doors were not yet opened. We had to spend one more miserable night here, and the last one together with our family. As if I had sensed it, all night I sat motionless so as not to wake my husband and son, who were sleeping with their heads on my shoulders. Although every part of my body was numb, I overcame my discomfort with a great effort of will and I held them both in an embrace – for the last time. Propping each other up, the young couple sat back to back on a suitcase, dozing. From time to time, one head or the other dropped and they were startled back to reality.

Saturday morning arrived, the morning of June 3. We had arrived at Auschwitz on Friday evening and the devout Jews had been praying from evening to morning; they had been besieging heaven in a lamenting tone, pleading and continuing to believe that the God of the Jews would help his "chosen" people.

I was no longer afraid of anything. I would have even gladly welcomed death just to be able to get out of the cattle car, which, even after everything I was yet to go through, remained one of my most degrading experiences. All of a sudden the doors were opened and we could take a deep breath of the morning air that rushed in. Instead of the scent of fresh air, however, our noses were assailed by a peculiar, nauseating odour. We looked at each other with alarm – it was only now, in the revealing light of day, that we saw what had become of us during the gruelling days. Unshaven men with pale, sunken faces, unkempt and haggard women crawled out of the cars, and from many, corpses and the insane, who had been travelling together with their relatives, were carried off. The latter were crying, wailing and sobbing hysterically, until they were quieted by a hard slap in the face.

Then men in striped clothes, obviously prisoners, stormed the train and demanded loudly in Polish, German and Yiddish that we leave everything behind and get out of the car empty-handed. I hung my sack of bread around my neck but it was roughly torn off by one of these screaming monsters in striped clothes. We got down from the car, robbed of everything, leaving behind our remaining belongings, papers, photos, cherished keepsakes. All that belonged to us, all that was left of our possessions, were the clothes on our backs. Even that was not for long.

We held tight to each other's hands so as not to lose one another, and I looked around for my mother and my sister and her family. I couldn't see anyone. All of a sudden, I felt my husband letting go of my hand and before I knew it both he and my son were torn away from us, disappearing into the crowd of men. From this we concluded, dejectedly, that men and women would be separated. Then we were lined up five in a row – oh, those rows of five! They will haunt us to the end of our days.

We started off. A German officer, a prime example of Germanic male beauty – as we found out later, Dr. Mengele, physician and hangman – stopped each and every row, smilingly scrutinized the five women, and with a wave of his hand, like a diabolical conductor, directed them to either the left or the right. At that point in time we didn't know that to the right, Life, and to the left, Death, would await us. This directing seemed to be done in a completely arbitrary fashion. Some older women, including myself, ended up grouped with the younger ones, while some healthy young women ended up on the left side together with the old, the sick and the weak. All the mothers with babies and with older children up to the age of twelve were directed to the left. I saw a friend of Ági's get off the train – the one in whose apartment she had spent her "honeymoon" – and in her arms was her gorgeous, cooing baby son, flailing his little fists. "Little Péter has been so well behaved," she called to us.

The Poles were whispering to some of the young mothers to hand over their children to the elderly women. They did not say why. What mother would be willing to part with her child? Only a few of them passed their children over to their mothers, and how they must have felt once they had opened their eyes to the truth.

One woman got off the train with her two children, four and five years of age. "Are they twins?" asked one of the Poles. "No," she answered. "Tell the doctor that they are twins," suggested the Pole, and she did. This woman is now back in Szatmár together with her children, who survived because twins were not killed, but were used as guinea pigs, for medical experiments.

We stood in front of Dr. Mengele. He directed Ágnes to the right; he looked at me and asked with a friendly smile whether I was able to walk. "Of course," I replied, and I was already on my way, holding my daughter's hand toward Life. But what kind of life! Given the anguish that awaited us, had we known about their fate, we might have envied those who ended up on the left side, whose time on earth concluded with a few cries of agony. But we had no idea about any of this. We imagined – or maybe we were even told by those people in striped clothes – that the young would be working and the old would be taking care of the children.

The group to which I was assigned (thanks to my much-criticized plumpness), started off toward the barracks, past the crossing gate, along with all the selected young women who were deemed able to work. That's when we saw, beyond the fence, women breaking rocks. Shaved completely bald, their heads bare under the burning sun, clad in motley, ill-fitting rags.

They approached the wire fence and, casting frightened glances around, screamed at us like the furies of hell to toss over our kerchiefs, bread, because everything would be confiscated. Those of us who still had such things started throwing them over, watching the women snatching them out of each other's hands, their faces reflecting hunger and suffering. Soon their overseers noticed this activity and started beating them, and we were prodded by the rifle butts of our German guards. We stopped throwing things.

We finally stopped at a building resembling a bathhouse. It was a disinfecting station. I looked around and was glad to see that the men were lined up not too far from us, in front of the entrance to a similar building. I spotted my loved ones among them. We couldn't converse, but I saw that each member of my immediate family was in the group with the young people. Only later would the significance of this fact become evident.

We were marched into a huge empty room. German women soldiers, with truncheons in their hands, ordered us to strip naked, place our clothes on the ground at the right and hold our shoes in our hands. We were then paraded in front of young Slovak women sitting in a row, who shaved our heads bald and then shaved our whole body. All of a sudden, pretty young girls and women turned into creatures of the underworld. It was impossible to recognize each other.

The whole time, German soldiers, mostly very young lads, walked up and down among us, staring and laughing at our suffering. Young women, their modesty assaulted, covered their faces. Our next stop was a room equipped with hot showers. This was welcome after the horrible train ride, but in a few minutes the showers were turned off and we had to dip our shoes in a tub filled with water; however, a German woman first checked if there were socks, money or jewellery hidden in them. If there were, the owner of the shoes was beaten with the truncheon. I saw bloody welts blossom all around me.

The next step was getting dressed. Surprisingly, we had to wear other people's rags instead of our own clothes. We had never seen anything of the kind and couldn't even imagine where they managed to get hold of them. I, for example, was sporting a floor-length dress made of cotton that had a grey design on a black background, with at least ten rows of ruffles at the hem, the neckline, and the sleeves. I stared at the awful garment in despair, though I was grateful for it later on. For weeks to come, I would tear off some of the ruffles and use them for handkerchiefs or toilet paper, thus finding a solution to one of our biggest problems. Eventually, the floor-length dress became a small garment reaching only to my knees. Ági and Zsófi, on the other hand, were given such short dresses that their bottoms showed, though they received long slips and even longer underwear.

We didn't know whether to laugh or cry when we saw each other in these carnival costumes. Our baldness made everyone look like an idiot, but somehow our brains had indeed grown dull as soon as we stepped onto the grounds of the camp. How were we to comprehend what had happened to us? We had lost our freedom, been stripped of all our feminine adornments, dressed in rags... we no longer had a gender or a name. We had become prisoners, *Häftlinge*. There was no way of telling what social class anyone had belonged to at home. This was true equality. We had all become the same wretched, accursed creatures. No one ever asked us for our names. We had become impersonal objects, machines in the hands of a cruel owner. A good owner protects his possessions from the rain, his animals from famine, but who was protecting us? Not even the good God above.

By the time we left the bathhouse, a cold rain had begun to fall. Each in just a single piece of clothing with underwear and a slip underneath, without a jacket, stockings or a kerchief, we got drenched. At the clothing distribution, a young Slovak woman (who was perhaps thinking of her own mother) had handed me a nice warm kerchief and whispered that I should hide it from the Germans' sight. I would bless her for it often. I did not dare to put it on just yet, and the rain streamed from our bald heads down our necks for hours.

Internment

We were lined up in rows of five and led into (as we found out later) Lager C, which lay beyond the wire fence. Before I progress any further in recording my memories, I have to explain what a Lager consisted of and who its leaders were. Lager C was one long, wide road lined with sixteen barracks, called blocks, which constituted our quarters. These blocks used to be stables for horses, as attested by the instructions for the care of horses written on plaques on the doors.

The Jewish leader of the Lager, called the *Lagerälteste*, was a woman from Nagymihály by the name of Magda. She was the most decent of our superiors; even though, at times, she hit us, she also cared about people and helped whenever she could. She and the *Schreiber*, scribes, who were chosen from among us, were staying at the *Schreibstube*, an administrative office where the official matters of the Lager were handled. They were, of course, given splendid treatment compared to us. One young woman, Lili Halász from Munkács, was so good and kind to everyone that she completely counterbalanced the actions of the others from Munkács. Not only could she help a lot of people, but she actually wanted to, and this was such a rarity.

Above the Jewish leader there were only Germans, male and female soldiers called *Aufseher*. Their superiors were called *Lagerführer*, then came the *Oberscharführer* and all the other kinds of *Führer*, most likely all the way up to the Father-Führer. All these *Führer* stood far above us, like pagan deities. Usually they only showed up at the roll call, or to decide our fate during the selection process.

Our immediate superiors were the Slovak women, the so-called *Blockälteste* or, as they were referred to in Slovak, *Blokova*. Each block had one of these sovereigns, and just as soldiers suffered most at the hands of sergeants and not those of generals and colonels, so we suffered most from the *Blokova* and the helpers chosen by them. Apart from this, only the *Stubendienst* team – the housekeeping crew – reigned over us.

The *Lagerälteste* was in charge of the administrative affairs of the Lager, while the Lager kapo was responsible for keeping order. It seems that the Germans selected the nastiest women for this job on purpose. The first one, Mrs. Pollák from Nagymihály, a greying woman with a pleasant face, and the next one, a girl from Humenné by the name of Szuri, were mean and cruel. They beat us so badly that everyone fled from them and feared them like the flames of hell.

There might be a mitigating, if not exculpating circumstance, in the defence of the cold-heartedness of the Slovak women: these young women had been dragged from their homes by the Nazis two years earlier, and some told us – to our immense horror – they had been sent to the front to service the soldiers. We hadn't wanted to believe these atrocities, but now we found out they were true. Most of them suffered through this miserable ordeal and were transported to Auschwitz once they became ill. What they must have been through, the human mind cannot grasp. Some had witnessed their friends being torn to pieces by dogs, which in those days used to be the favourite sport of the henchmen of the SS.

When the transports of Slovak women arrived at Auschwitz in the spring of 1942, they were assigned to brutal forced labour. A few months later, they were moved to the new camp at Birkenau and were assigned to heavy construction work like demolishing houses to build new barracks and blocks, and constructing the roads. In these early days of the camp, they were sleeping in a stable, they couldn't wash themselves and there was no toilet. There were plenty of lice, itch mites, filth and typhus, which carried out such devastation that hundreds of their companions, relatives and siblings were transferred to the crematorium every day.

Small wonder that these women had lost all human feeling. They were not interested in anything in the world apart from themselves. Never for a moment did they believe that they would ever get out from behind the electrified fences. Each one of them had a Polish friend who supplied them with everything they needed. Over the years, they had been shaved bald so many times as a punishment that, when they were finally allowed to, they grew beautiful wavy hair and had lovely hairdos. That's what we envied the most, we women with our dreadful bald heads. They were elegant, groomed and pretty, and it's not surprising that they considered themselves queens among us, who were nothing but an unkempt, tattered, dirty mess.

We had to wait only a few hours in the rain, which was very fortunate; some groups had been kept in the latrine for two or three days before being assigned to different blocks. The blocks were already filled with the people who had arrived from Lower Carpathia a few weeks prior.

A short, pretty, cat-eyed woman with a sly face and a fantastic hairdo, clad in a raincoat, appeared in front of our troop. She counted off ten rows and led us to Block 3. We found ourselves in a huge long room with some sort of an antechamber. This opened on to the *Blokova's* room, to the right, and on to the so-called *Brotkammer*, bread chamber, to the left, which was occupied by the *Blokova's* personal staff, a chambermaid, cook and others.

Near the entrance to the giant block stood a stove decorated with a silk kerchief and a flower vase. This was the crowning glory of the whole block. The heating flue emanating from it, encased in painted red brick, ran the length of the block. One of the *Stubendienst* was assigned the task of polishing it from morning to night. If only we had been given such good care as this *Heizung*, heater, was.

On either side of the *Heizung* were metre-wide passages, and beside them were our living spaces: three-tier bunk beds. These were our homes – at least for those who got one. Everyone was trying to find a place on the bunk beds, to get some rest after the dreadful day, but the original occupants rebuffed these attempts. We didn't push or shove, so neither Ági nor myself nor another young woman, Mrs. Bandi Glück, managed to find a place. We stood around until exhaustion overcame us and we slumped down on the bare floor in the tiny nook at the end, not caring anymore.

We envied those who had found a space even though about twelve people occupied each tier, which was the size of a double bed. Each person got fifteen or twenty centimetres of space that comprised rough planks of this width. In order to facilitate cleaning, the bunk bed was made up of movable planks, with cracks in between them that cut red stripes into people's sides. People lay on completely bare boards and every six persons had to share a grey blanket or a raggedy quilt for a cover. Everyone used their shoes as a pillow under their head because shoes were such an irreplaceable treasure that this was the only way to keep them safe. We all felt for them many times during the night to make sure they hadn't been stolen.

Every so often I heard screaming and yelling from a bunk bed falling on those sleeping underneath, crushing them. In that moment, however, we were eyeing the beds with longing as we sat on the bare floor, glistening with puddles of water, the rain pouring on us incessantly. It could serve as some small consolation that we were not the only ones getting wet; throughout the block, the rain fell through the gaps in the wooden roof. The middle and lower bunks were at least somewhat protected.

As newcomers, we were objects of unrelenting hatred. Our placement was supervised by fifteen screaming women dressed in grey prison garb and equipped with cudgels. They all looked as if they had been hangmen or dogcatchers in their former lives. Their voices were completely hoarse, raw and husky from all the screaming, and I can't even describe how scared I was of them. All of a sudden, I spotted a familiar face among them. Could this screaming, flogging, scary creature, devoid of all human attributes, really be Dr. Markovics, a lawyer and an excellent musician from Szatmár? It was her! I then started to realize that the *Stubendienst* were women just like us, who had known better days.

The *Stubendienst* was made up mostly of women from Máramaros and Lower Carpathia who had arrived a few weeks earlier than us. Their job was to tidy up the block, wash the floor three times a day, distribute dinner and do the washing up, but of course within two or three days they farmed out this work to those who were happy to carry it out for a little bit of extra food. Instead, they spent their days buying clothes in exchange for food from those pretty girls who got hold of these items from guys who mysteriously managed to toss them over the fence. The men obtained these items from the inmates' clothing warehouse situated near the crematorium, which unfortunately was an inexhaustible source. These young women ruled over us and most of them abused their position. The eighteen to twenty members of the *Stubendienst* filled the role of ministers, but not in a democratic system. Our heads were spinning by the time we figured out the "power structure."

We were crouching on the floor, doing our best to avoid the raindrops when some members of the *Stubendienst* shouted at us, "Get outside! Zählappell!" (Roll call!) Of course we didn't have the faintest idea what it was all about, but since we saw that everyone was in a great rush, scrambling over one another to get outside, we thought that something pleasant was about to happen, and we went too. After all, it didn't really matter whether we got wet inside or outside.

Once outside we were made to form up in rows of five, permanently this time. Apart from Ági and myself, our row consisted of Mrs. Bandi Glück, my niece Kató, and her governess, who luckily got grouped with us. After this first *Appell*, every day for the five months we stayed in Auschwitz we had to stand for *Appell* at dawn, with the stars and the moon still in the sky, and every afternoon, no matter the weather, even when we were sick or feverish.

The *Appell* meant being counted by the Germans, but this was not as simple as it sounds. First, for an hour or two, the rows were arranged and rearranged by our *Vertreter*, representative, and members of the *Stubendienst*. When we were finally standing in proper order, the *Blokova* made her entrance, declaring that if anyone dared to utter a sound or make a movement during *Appell*, she would be done for. After she had walked up and down among our rows, dispensing a few slaps across the face to those who were not standing properly according to her, she counted us several times. After a further hour, the Germans arrived at last, both male and female soldiers, and we were alerted to this by a shout of "Achtung!" (Attention!) At this point, we stood there like frozen statues while they counted us with grim faces, because the smallest movement would incite their anger, and then the ever-present dog whip would swing into action.

The names of these women soldiers were Irma Grese, Hasse, Drechsler and Brunner, and with the exception of Grese, they all reminded me of horses. Drechsler had long teeth protruding from her short-lipped horse face; thick-set Hasse, whose very name exuded hatred, reminded me of a clumsy Mecklenburg horse, with her piano legs; while Brunner, with her petite figure and flowing mane, brought to mind a little pony. But Irma Grese, the German woman who took the roll call on that first day, was cut from a different cloth.

I will never forget the moment I first laid eyes on her. An angel descending from heaven couldn't have looked more beautiful. Her golden hair was pulled back in a bun, she had the most gorgeous dark blue eyes I had ever seen, and her gleaming teeth, dimpled cheeks and pretty figure were in such harmony, so perfect, that for a moment I had the impression that I was in a movie theatre and the prima donna had appeared on the screen. She wore a pair of well-tailored greenish-grey culottes with a snow-white blouse and had an army jacket thrown over her shoulders. She would always come by bicycle, with an army hat tilted at a stylish angle atop her shiny hair, holding yellow pigskin gloves in one hand and a horsewhip in the other, sporting a pair of pretty patent-leather boots on her feet. Hard lines would appear on her lovely forehead as she strode past us to deal some poor *Häftling* a blow with her horsewhip if she didn't like something about her. On these occasions, her ever-so-lovely face would become contorted with rage, but shortly after, she would turn to the *Blokova* with an angelic smile, because those two were fast friends. That is to say, she used the *Blokova's* room to try on the suits, the lingerie, and indeed anything that was sewn for her by an excellent seamstress in Block 3 originally from Munkács. Although she was very friendly with the *Blokova*, this did not preclude the latter from uttering dreadful curses at her as soon as her back was turned. Once, this beautiful beast kicked a girl to death right in front of our eyes.

The male soldiers could all speak Hungarian; some of them were from Temesvár, and there was even one from Szatmár, registered under the name Urbanowszky. They were always drunk. Sometimes the women were, too, but while the men were counting us they were reeling about or just pretending to count us. On the other hand, they were not pretending to beat us – they laid that on lavishly.

Grese, the angel-faced devil, together with a few of her cohorts, counted all 32,000 or so occupants of the Lager. This served strictly as a means of torturing us because how could any one of us have been missing? The Lager was surrounded by a high-voltage electric wire fence, and only those ready to kill themselves ventured near it, which was an everyday occurrence. It was impossible to escape, so why was it then necessary to count us twice a day, morning and afternoon? As long as the numbers were right, there was no problem, but woe to us if the *Appell* numbers were off. At such times, we did not get away with merely standing in the rain for three or four hours. Instead, the whole Lager had to kneel until they managed to figure out, after re-counting two or three times, where they had made an error. They were warmly dressed, never caring that we would be shivering from the cold, suffering exhaustion and starvation, for a few more hours.

One time, when a fourteen-year-old girl had fallen asleep and was not present for *Appell*, causing a shortfall in the numbers, we were kept kneeling from four in the afternoon until midnight. The horse-faced Drechsler, baring her protruding teeth, dragged the girl, who had been found in the meantime, by means of a crook around her neck, transporting her straight to the crematorium.

The *Appell* was followed by the distribution of supper and we had to wait outside for this as well, at times almost collapsing from exhaustion. The meal consisted of twenty decagrams of bread and either two decagrams of margarine or a slice of *Wurst,* a piece of cheese or a spoonful of jam. All of this food seemed artificially made, nothing was real, but it still tasted good to us. However, on this first evening, we newcomers did not receive any supper. We weren't hungry anyways, so filled with the day's horrors that we would not have been able to eat.

At last, we returned to the block, some of us, like me, to sit in puddles of water again to have our rest. Then the *Blokova* entered – the one we were supposed to call Miss – and stepped up onto the heating flue to give a speech. Its content went something like this: "You idiots! I call you that because that's what you are for letting yourself be hauled to this place, when you knew very well that half of Europe's Jewry had been deported. [I had to agree with her completely, and I acknowledged that she was a bright and intelligent woman.] That's why we Slovak Jews hate you Hungarian Jews so much, because for years you've been sleeping under comforters, sitting around tables covered with white cloths, while we were being tortured to death and torn apart by dogs and you never came to our rescue. [How?] We buried, rather, we transferred, our family members to the crematorium. We are the only survivors of eight- to ten-member families and there is no sympathy or pity left in us. We hate you because you are not going to spend four years here, the way we've had to, because this war cannot possibly go on that long. But none of you should count on getting out of here alive because there isn't a single instance of this happening at Auschwitz. We're also going to die like dogs here after many years of suffering, but so will you."

We looked at each other in anguish. Where had we ended up? What would become of us? Then my niece Kató risked a question. "Miss, when are we going to see our mothers and loved ones?" With utter composure, the *Blokova* answered, "Don't you ever ask such stupid questions again. Look outside! Your mothers and all those who are not with you are going up in smoke to the sky. All those who were not grouped with you, the young ones able to do work, were killed in the gas chambers and burnt in the crematorium."

Stunned at this horrible, heartless revelation, we just stared down blankly, our minds paralyzed. No, this was impossible to believe. Weren't we living in the twentieth century? We could never have thought the Germans capable of such a thing, a "cultured nation" shamelessly trampling all culture into the mud.

Howls, sobs and wails arose as we woke to the horrifying reality that we had said goodbye to our loved ones forever. "What are you howling about?" shouted the Miss. "You also will end up as smoke soon. It really doesn't matter whether it's sooner or later. You'd better realize that this is a Vernichtungslager – it was built for the annihilation of the prisoners – and the only way to leave it is by being transported for labour. Don't worry about being selected for this, the ones chosen should be happy. Although we haven't heard any news from those who've been taken away and we don't know what has become of them, anywhere must be better than here, alongside of the gas chamber and crematorium."

This was our reception from Ms. Klein, *Blokova* from Poprád, the chief of Block 3. She then called our attention to the fact that this was an exemplary block, where she would not tolerate any disorder, and that we had better take care of ourselves while our health held out. Then she exited haughtily.

Meanwhile it had turned dark and, at our imploring, one of the

Stubendienst, Olga Züszmann from Halmi, took pity on us poor souls who hadn't managed to get a bed. She gave us two pallets with no stuffing and two blankets for us to sleep on, on the wet floor. My dear little daughter snuggled up to me and this was such a sweet, reassuring feeling, but at the same time it was terrible to witness each other's suffering. She would soon be sobbing, seeing me on my knees for the first time. The other daughters kept consoling themselves: how fortunate that our mothers did not end up here; we could not bear to see them kneel down, and we would die if ever someone slapped them in the face. Even then, I realized that the only thing one could not survive is one's own death. We were both stronger than iron and weaker than a speck of dust.

We cried ourselves to sleep after the sufferings of the terrible day and we woke with our hearts racing at three in the morning, at the sound of awful shouting. "Aufstehen!" (Get up!) "Quickly, quickly! Get coffee!"

As no one was keen on the idea of jumping out of their warm little nest in the dark, cold night to carry the terribly heavy cauldrons, the *Stubendienst* started yelling again and striking at people with sticks. In reaction to these blows, sixty women dragged themselves to their feet to go and get coffee. We had to get up right away as well and rush to the latrine because by the time they came back we were supposed to be standing in rows of five in the yard, waiting for the heavenly libation.

The *Stubendienst* dispensed the coffee in one common dish for all five of us in our row. Everyone, at least those who had the stomach for it, drank from it, not having individual dishes or spoons. The rest of us became nauseous and were unable to drink the bitter swill even though it had one great advantage: it was hot. We were chilled to the bone in the June dawn. We wrapped the blankets around us, under our clothing, which would earn us a terrible beating if noticed, to stop ourselves from shivering. Still, many of us were incapable of drinking, no matter how much we longed for some hot liquid.

After *Appell*, three hundred strong women were picked from among us for rock-breaking detail. Nobody took the rock breaking seriously, as there was no need for it at all, yet it was still awful to sit outside in the heat or the rain for hours and break rocks that would stubbornly resist the efforts of amateurs.

The rest of us had nothing else to do until lunch but lie on the *Kojen*, the bunks, in the block. Ági and I didn't even have a place to sit during the day because our little nook was used for storing blankets. So we wandered around outside or in the block, until, after a few days, my legs were swollen to three times their size and I couldn't even stand. The same *Stubendienst* member who had given us the blanket the first night gave us a place on one of the *Kojen* that had been vacated by someone ill. Ági and I occupied the place of one person, so my resting place was a fifteen-centimetre board that proved to be a somewhat tight fit for my hundred-and-fifty-five-pound body. At least I could stretch my aching, swollen legs. I had a "home." Poor Mrs. Bandi Glück was not assigned a place for weeks; her legs, back and kidneys were aching, since she never managed to get a good night's rest.

The first lunch arrived. Steaming in cauldrons was a thick, yellowish-grey concoction, made out of dried turnips, that one could not call food, even with the best of intentions. In it you could find plenty of stones, bromide, I'm sure, and pieces of wood. Surely sand must have been one of the ingredients in the recipe. Using a small spoon-like thing carved of wood that someone had lent us, we tasted the dish, but pushed away the plate assigned to the five of us in disgust. In a few days our eyes were hollow from hunger, yet for long weeks to come we were unable to eat. Others were eating away, and rightly so – it was a declaration of wanting to live and, albeit with eyes closed, they ate any amount that they could get hold of. Zsófi would first finish her lunch in her own block and then come over to ours and gladly eat up our portions as well.

I really don't know what kept Ági and me alive during these weeks.

All we ate was the bread and what was served with it at suppertime. We saved half of it for the morning and that's all the food we had all day. We were losing weight day by day but we could afford it; we were both strong. A very sad fate awaited those who were severely debilitated. More and more, people got diarrhea, which they tried to cure by not eating. This weakened them so much that during selection they could have easily ended up among those condemned to death. My advice to anyone with diarrhea was to eat as much as she could and pay no heed to it and indeed, in many cases the sick person recovered, not deteriorating as much as those who refused to eat.

The miserable days kept passing. I no longer had any idea what day of the week or month it was. The season turned into summer. Although the dawns remained chilly and we suffered from the cold during the early morning *Appell*, by contrast, during the afternoon *Appell* we were fainting from the hellish heat. Well, there was no reason to complain of monotony.

Initially, when a woman collapsed at our side due to the heat or hunger, we hollered for water – we were not allowed to step out of formation even if someone died beside us – at which point the *Blokova* would scream angrily, "Why are you making such a big deal out of a fainting spell? You idiots, she will come to on her own. If she kicks the bucket, so what, I have seen worse calamities." We listened, devastated, to this display of indifference and callousness, but as the weather grew hotter and more and more people fainted, we too became less sensitive to the suffering of others. That's when we started to understand how years of horrible suffering had killed all human feeling in the Slovak women.

Our *Blokova* wasn't even one of the worst. She was rough, but she cared about people's welfare. She made sure that we got our food on time and that not much was stolen from it beforehand. Number 3 was indeed an exemplary block. She kept order and discipline, checked everything, and on a few occasions even distributed the food herself.

The *Blokova*'s retinue in Number 3 consisted of the following people: her assistant, Médi; Szuri, who was in charge of her personal needs; and a personal cook. Médi, the wife of a lawyer from Nagyszőlős, was a rather tall, strong brunette. On arrival, she had left her beautiful three-year-old daughter with her mother, and had been grouped with the young women. She had become extremely embittered when she learned the truth, and in trying to forget her sorrows, she started working in the block, scrubbing floors and cleaning. The *Blokova* took a liking to her and picked her as her assistant. What a stroke of luck for her! This was like being a prime minister. She slept in the *Blokova*'s room, could eat as much as she wanted, and was even given some clothes. The more courageous ones would turn to her when they wanted something – we could not speak directly to the Miss unless asked to. Such is the custom with queens.

Szuri was an immensely coarse and vulgar girl. She cleaned, washed and ironed for the *Blokova*, and also served as her bosom buddy. Walking around arm in arm, giggling, she informed and influenced the *Blokova* in every matter, and perhaps this was the reason why they had absolutely no tolerance for anyone with intelligence.

The cook worked only for the *Blokova*, and her job was to prepare as diverse menus as possible from the rather monotonous provisions. However, if the German women soldiers noticed that there was cooking going on in the block, all the *Blokova* were made to participate in sport. Sport served as a punishment and consisted of having to do the most unpleasant exercises for one or two hours: leapfrog, dropping to the ground on command, running with huge rocks in their hands, and similar activities that they dreaded. We dreaded them just as much because it went without saying that afterwards they would exact their revenge on us. Otherwise, we would have taken pleasure in watching the torturing of our torturers. Still, we were outraged when a German soldier slapped our *Blokova* around for a minor transgression one time, right in front of our eyes.

So the cook, to avoid detection, prepared meals at night. We enviously eyed the croquettes made out of grated raw potatoes and fried in margarine. It was our keenest desire to get hold of one of these, but this was out of the question. The families of the maid and the cook were amply supplied; we kept losing weight and they were putting it on. Needless to say, losing weight represented a mortal peril – the crematorium.

When someone got sick, she could finish her life on this earth without getting so much as an aspirin, because when we arrived in Auschwitz-Birkenau our Lager didn't even have a pharmacy or an infirmary, despite the presence of a lot of physicians in our ranks. Furthermore, the Hungarian Jews had brought enough medicine with them to stock at least ten pharmacies. We figured that most of these medications had been shipped to Germany for the soldiers.

One day, physicians were suddenly selected to set up an infirmary. As I was watching the group of women leaving for rock-breaking detail, I spotted Ilonka Bernát among them, the pharmacist from Avasfelsőfalu who had treated us to such a lovely afternoon snack the day we were forced off the train for lack of proper papers. Now she was a pitiful sight, with her bald head, her thin, almost yellow face, her tiny body clad in a child's skirt that didn't even come down to her knees.

"My dear Ilonka, are you about to break rocks even though you are a pharmacist?" I commiserated. "Not for long," she answered with a happy smile. "Soon the pharmacy will be opened up and the head pharmacist has promised to put me in charge there." I was smiling to myself at her naivety, since you couldn't believe anything the Germans promised, or even expect its opposite to be true. I didn't believe that she would be the person picked for this job because the Germans always chose heavily built women for any job or position. However, everything happened differently from what one would expect in a logical world, and before long a tidy woman dressed in a snow-white cloak with a pretty kerchief on her head appeared before me. I had great difficulty recognizing my friend Ilonka in this woman.

The pharmacy was soon in operation, with pretty furniture

painted white and a curtained-off triple bed for the three people who stayed in the pharmacy: Ilonka; the gorgeous pharmacist Éva Citrom from Marosvásárhely; and Baba Böhm, the sweet little girl from Székelyudvarhely who worked as a chambermaid. In fact, she was a French teacher with a university education, and her mother was a physician in the Lager.

Beautiful Éva was the best-looking woman in the whole Lager, and she walked among us dressed in milky white, like a white swan among bald chicks. She received a constant supply of the best food and clothes from her men friends. In effect, these three women had the best luck. They did not have to participate in *Appell* and nobody ordered them around. The only person they feared was Mengele and the others in charge of selections. They supplied the *Blokova* with cosmetics and medicine, their favour returned by entire cartons of cheese, whole sticks of salami and pots of honey. This was our good fortune, because Ilonka used some of this supply to feed Ági and me. Thus the starvation, which was starting to take on grave proportions, came to an end. She couldn't give us much, having several relatives and friends whom she had to help, but even this little extra was sufficient to assuage our constant, brutal hunger.

I received some medicine from her, painkillers, for my rheumatic legs; otherwise, I couldn't have managed to stand six to eight hours a day. I passed on the surplus medicine to those in need, and not in exchange for bread as others did. I was glad to be able to help. When we arrived in Auschwitz we became as poor as church mice, and my greatest regret was that I, who always used to help those in need, was powerless. Not being able to give to others hurt me more than not having anything myself.

Life in Auschwitz

After a few weeks, the *Vertreter* noticed how diligently Ági was carrying the heavy cauldrons, and the *Blokova* assigned her to *Stubendienst* duty. She had attained a desired position, and she demonstrated that it was possible to keep order and discipline with kind words, that it was not necessary to be rude and to hit people just because she was "above" them.

Shortly after, when people from the Transdanubian region arrived in Auschwitz, they occupied the four *Kojen* under Ági's care. They practically worshipped Ági. She listened to their complaints, tried to fulfill all their requests and helped them as best she could. She managed to procure medicine when they were sick and she applied a bandage to an older woman with a hernia. They were so grateful for every little thing and happy if they could be of any help to Ági.

We obtained a splendid sleeping place because the *Stubendienst* had their own *Kojen* right beside the door. They slept five or six to a tier instead of twelve, and under fine silk quilts. They had "organized," namely stolen, them from the warehouse opposite. It was in these warehouses that the Germans stored the many quilts and other bed linens, and they requisitioned about twenty women from Block 3 to attend to them. They had of course already meticulously searched the quilts and most likely found a lot of jewellery and other things sewn inside, but the girls in charge of the warehouse carried out yet another inspection – to their own benefit naturally – and even they found a lot of valuables in them, but mostly cloth. They exchanged these things for food with the *Stubendienst*, who used them to dress well.

Actually, the *Blokova* insisted that the *Stubendienst* be presentable. They had the seamstresses sew them pretty aprons out of the pillowcases that originated from the warehouse as well; we never figured out what they did with the down from the pillows. This warehouse was also home to all the pots and pans that were brought along by those naive people who thought they would be cooking for their families in the deportation. Once, I was called in to help with washing up these pots and pans. What a joy! Right away, I tied a whole duvet cover around myself, and I kept it on when I left. Ági managed to have a pretty *Stubendienst* apron made from it. I was delighted to steal from the Germans.

Ilonka, the pharmacist, bought us warm sweaters as a present, which meant we were no longer as cold during the morning *Appell*. We had a good bed with pleasant bedmates, and so our situation started to become bearable. We shared our bed with the lawyer from Szatmár and her *Stubendienst* sister, a physician from Kolozsvár; Dr. Ilona Ligeti; and Anna Szász, the energetic and industrious, well-known *Dreckkapo* who undertook cleaning the latrine and *Waschraum*, and was tasked with controlling the stampede there. Her job back home had been nothing like this at all – she used to earn her living as a piano teacher. She organized the latrine and *Waschraum* teams, whose members had a tag bearing the initials "WC" sewn on their clothes, to indicate that they were not ordinary mortals but individuals with an illustrious occupation.

The first time I entered the WC, my eyes grew wide with astonishment. It was the oddest thing. It was a block just like all the others, but it featured three extremely long benches made of cement, each containing three hundred seats. In this way, nine hundred women at a time could, and did, attend to their bodily needs. It was horrible to get used to doing it in public. There were three such WCs in the

Lager – accommodating twenty-seven hundred men and women at a time – but even so, you risked your life trying to get in and out of this place. Everybody was trying to do their business before *Appell* because no matter what happened while we were standing there for a couple of hours – and often something did happen – no one was allowed to leave the formation. At such times, it was hard to get into the WC without breaking an arm or a leg.

I signed up for the *Waschraum* team because I realized that it was much better to work and move about freely all day rather than lying around on the bed, which would weaken a person considerably. I became the doorkeeper and saw to it that people did not trample one another. Men cleaned the interiors of the WCs, and I was greatly surprised when among these workers I recognized Dr. Sándor Singer, the distinguished heart specialist from Szatmár. So this was the type of "health care work" doctors were used for. The women were responsible for keeping the benches clean, and I must say exemplary order and cleanliness prevailed.

Actually, the WC gained the status of a sort of place of entertainment, as the only place where the occupants of the different blocks could meet. This is where people discussed the goings on in their blocks, but there would be trouble if, during this socializing, the terror of the WCs, whom we called "Piroska" (Little Red Riding Hood) on account of her red hair, burst onto the scene. She was a very young woman, not yet twenty, and she had been living in captivity for four years. She had narrowly escaped the gas chamber three times. Once, in the winter, she had jumped off the vehicle that was transporting her there. She spent the night outdoors, unconscious, and by morning both her breasts had been frostbitten. From everything that she had endured, it is little wonder that her mind was affected. She had become a sadist and, armed with a big stick, she would burst into the WC several times a day, rushing through the place and striking at the naked behinds of hundreds of women sitting there, in order to drive them out.

In spite of all this, the various liaisons between male and female workers also took place in the WC. The venue – shall we say – was somewhat unusual, but in a few weeks' time, no one was bothered by it. I often saw workers having a hearty meal in the WC. The women who worked there were soon dressed in smart clothing, having obtained it all from the male workers.

In my *Waschraum*, the workers were of a high calibre – there was an opera singer from Vienna with an enchanting voice who used to scrub the wash basins to the sweet sounds of *La traviata* or *Rigoletto*. The heart-rending sounds opened the floodgates of my feelings, and tears started pouring from my eyes. Things were only bearable as long as we didn't allow anything to touch our souls, as long as we worried only about having enough to eat.

I usually sat by the back door, listening to the moving melodies, looking over at the mortuary of the neighbouring Czech Lager. Typhus was raging among the Czechs and sometimes in the course of an hour, thirty or forty corpses were carried out, draped with grey blankets, their yellow stick-like legs and the waxy soles of their feet jutting out in deathly rigour. At the beginning I was so disturbed by this awful sight that I couldn't even eat, but I got used to it. However, I still shudder when I remember the cart that used to stop in front of the mortuary around noon, loaded with uncovered naked corpses piled on top of each other – men, women and children.

The Czech Lager used to be the object of our envy. There, the families – men, women, children and the elderly – were allowed to live together, and apparently no selections had been made because there were even some invalids in wheelchairs among them. Compared to us they were doing extremely well; they were dressed in their own clothes and their hair was not shorn. Then, one day during a July *Appell* we saw that there was a big selection going on among the Czechs. Young women and men were separated out and immediately taken away in a transport. From that day on, those left behind were not given anything to eat. They were condemned to death, a waste to feed. In a few days their eyes grew hollow from hunger. They perished by the hundreds every day, allegedly from typhus, but in reality they starved to death. They were begging for food and we tried to sneak some food under the fence to them, at least what we could spare, given our meagre supply, at the risk of being shot by the guard high up in the tower, who never left his post. One young woman was indeed shot and killed, and another lost an eye to a bullet.

I can still see a shrivelled-up little old woman, her withered face framed by tangled grey locks, as she reached for a piece of bread with a shaking hand and gave it to her grandchild; she watched with hungry eyes, moving her mouth as if she too were eating, while the little one was chewing it. It was a heart-wrenching sight.

One evening, the Germans ordered a strict *Blocksperre*. This meant that both entrances to each block were locked and no one was allowed to leave. We waited to find out what was coming, suspecting something bad. All of a sudden, the deathly silence of the still night was interrupted by dreadful screaming, yelling, wailing and the barking of dogs. This went on for hours, and we covered our ears so as not to hear the agonized cries.

It happened to be a very hot evening. The air inside the block was stifling and we could hardly wait for the doors to be opened so that we could breathe some fresh air. At last, silence enveloped the Lager and the doors were opened. From my bed, I witnessed a gruesome drama. Three Lagers away, in front of our gate, stood one of the crematoria. Flames were erupting from its chimney, reaching high into the sky. The whole area was flooded with light as bright as day, as if ravaged by an immense conflagration. It continued like this all night. Nobody could sleep. We cried the whole night through, our hearts trembling. The Czechs had met their fate. The following day, their Lager was completely empty. We were nauseous for days from the smell of burnt flesh and fat that permeated the air. You can imagine how we felt after every new selection from that day on.

There could be no doubt in our minds anymore about what we

had refused to believe in the beginning. Our *Blokova* was right – we would not leave this place alive.

~

We had been in Auschwitz for just over a month when I saw a cart on the street of the Lager drawn by men in striped clothing instead of horses. Zsófi's husband was among them. I ran to fetch Zsófi, who came and sat down on the ground beside the cart as if she were breaking rocks, to be able to exchange a few words with her husband. I followed suit, but the men were being guarded by a German with a cocked rifle, and therefore he could only mention in a few words that he was staying with my husband and János. They were being treated very badly but they were healthy, and they would be transferred elsewhere in a few days. They were housed in Lager A behind the Czech Lager and if, after *Appell*, we were to stand on a hill, they would come to the wire and we could see each other.

We felt so excited, waiting for the prearranged hour to arrive. Of course, we couldn't make out their faces, but the characteristic shapes were still recognizable, especially my lanky son with his sleeves barely covering his elbows. The three of them were also standing on a hill and János, overjoyed to see us, started jumping and waving with the typical wild movements of a teenager. We were crying and laughing at the sight of the familiar movements, happy to see them, even in this limited way.

Later that day we received a "letter," a few words written on a piece of wood. My husband wrote that Ági's husband, Pali, had also been with them for a few days, until one day, while they were in the WC, Pali was taken away in a transport. Both of them were really fond of the dear boy and were very disheartened. Ági cried and grieved and was inconsolable. We managed to have one of our letters reach my husband because the liquidated Czech Lager was filled by a few thousand of our group and they facilitated the correspondence. Then one day, we received a farewell letter from Zoltán. My blessed, caring, good husband wrote that the train that was going to transport them was already in the station, and as far as they knew they were to work in a mine in Mährisch-Ostrau. They hoped we would see each other again in this life, but he was under the impression that we would be spending the winter here. He suggested we try to get hold of some warmer clothes.

Oh, that farewell letter! How many times I reread it, until its lines, which I knew by heart, were worn away completely by my tears. How many nights I spent crying quietly, making sure not to be heard, not to burden Ági with my sorrow. I sensed we would never see one another again. It was still summer, yet we had suffered from the cold already – what would happen when autumn came, and the harsh winter? We would not survive it, that was for sure. Neither my husband nor my one-hundred-eighty-centimetre-tall, skinny son would be able to endure it. I felt certain that this farewell letter was final and that I was saying goodbye to my dear ones. Ági was most likely tormented by the same kind of thoughts, but she didn't say anything and neither did I. We kept looking at each other with encouraging smiles, even when our hearts were about to break.

The days kept passing, and compared to the others we were doing all right. Ágnes, being in the *Stubendienst*, got more food, which was more palatable since it had a few potatoes in it as well. They were thrown in unpeeled and we had to spit out the peels, which often took away our appetite, but I solved the problem by removing the potatoes from the soup, peeling them with my fingers, and then mashing them together with a bit of margarine, which resulted in a heavenly dish. We received double portions for supper as well, and sometimes Ilonka would also give us a few tasty morsels; not only were we not starving, we were even able to pass some of our food on to others. Zsófi, who had been assigned to a different block, was starving terribly and was losing weight at an alarming rate. We managed to smuggle her into our block and get her weight back up in a few weeks. She also got some food in exchange for sewing.

Meanwhile, all through the summer, the Germans had been separating out the strong and healthy young people. This took place after *Appell*, which meant standing around for an additional few hours. I usually stood beside Ági, in with the *Stubendienst*, but on one occasion I inadvertently ended up with the "common folk." As luck would have it, all of a sudden Mengele, Grese and Drechsler arrived and began the selection. Poor Ági, scared to death that I would be taken away, sprang out of formation, which was considered a capital offence, and rushed over to me, asking me to stand beside her because they wouldn't make a selection from among the *Stubendienst*. The *Blokova*, right on her heels, asked Ági angrily why she had left the formation. "I've come to fetch my mom," she answered, "so we won't be separated." "If you ran over to your mom, you might as well stay with her – I have no need of a Stubendienst who would leave the formation for her mom," she responded haughtily.

Ági remained by my side. I held the hand of Kató Wohl, my niece; her governess and Mrs. Bandi Glück were the other two people in our row. All four of them were selected, but I wasn't. Seeing Ági's desperate face, I looked imploringly at Drechsler of the terrible reputation, and risked these words: "My daughter." Wonder of wonders, Drechsler pardoned us. "Let her stay too," she said amiably. But when the next mother, encouraged by what she'd seen, stated that she'd also like to stay with her daughter, she received two slaps on the face that caused her to fall down, and they got separated out of spite. Everything was a matter of luck there. You could not count on anything; everything happened differently from how one might have imagined.

We stayed together once again, which made us both very happy, but Ági lost her job on account of me and, together with those few who stayed behind, we were transferred into another block, number 9. Being assigned to a new block meant starting over from scratch. This was a great blow. Previously, six of us had been sleeping on one bunk. Now, however, we were squeezed together with ten strangers. There was no longer any extra food, and we really needed Ilonka's support. To top it all off, Ági came down with a fever and since she was afraid of reporting it, she stood for *Appell* with a fever of 39.5 degrees Celsius as long as she was able. Eventually, she collapsed.

Everyone was extremely scared of the infirmary because Mengele and other "doctors" often carried out selections there. He would have the weak ones loaded onto a cart, and help them to their "eternal recovery." Every now and then, we saw this cart, loaded with the condemned. In spite of all this, Ilonka made Ági enter the infirmary, promising that she'd be on the lookout and hide her in the pharmacy in case of trouble. Ági had a mild case of pneumonia that would have been the end of anyone else, but Ilonka took care of her and fed her, and in eight days the fever was gone. She still had a nasty cough, and so she stayed at the infirmary – until Mengele arrived. Ilonka sent her back to Block 9 in haste. She was awfully weak when she returned, just in time for the season of starvation in the new block.

Even apart from this we were having a bad time of it in this messy block. The *Blokova*, Editke, was the twenty-one-year-old daughter of a baker from Rozsnyó. By her own admission, at the age of seventeen she had been transported to the front by the Germans for the amusement of the soldiers, and she spent a year there, wearing a sign on her back that described her profession.

In Auschwitz, Editke had a boyfriend, a Polish prisoner, and nothing else in the whole world interested her. We didn't see her all day because she was either lying down, being given massages or manicures, or having her hair done. Her only action in the evening, before receiving her boyfriend or going to sleep, was to storm through the block in a lacy, pink silk nightgown, which the rest of us could only dream of, and strike at anyone in her way with a big stick. "Lagerruhe! Lagerruhe!" (Quiet!) she screamed, the battle cry that signalled bedtime. Her friend from Bustyaháź, the infamous and pugnacious Katica, also armed with a stick, followed her and beat whomever she missed. Then, a mean Polish *Vertreter* also struck at us unfortunate, exhausted women.

We slowly got to know the *Stubendienst* here as well. While in Number 3 they were women from Lower Carpathia, here they were from Nyíregyháza. Among them were several intelligent women who spoke to us like normal human beings. We made friends with them, and obtained better beds and more pleasant neighbours later on, but we were starving. In contrast, the finest meals were being prepared in the block for Editke and her six-member retinue. A thousand people with growling stomachs, faint from hunger, could smell the various fine aromas, and that's when I understood how hunger could drive a person to steal or kill.

By the time we got used to Block 9, it got vacated. In August, thousands of people from the Lodz ghetto were deported to Auschwitz and many were placed there. It was terrible to be dropped into new surroundings again, to get to know new people, to gain their favour. Once again, Ilonka came to our rescue. She found us a place in the workers' block, Number 14. This block had the reputation of having no selections, but to get a place there, one first needed to be assigned to the workers' team in the office. There, they were constantly trying to create new work opportunities to save as many people as possible from selection.

I became a gardener. Each block had a plot two metres long by one metre wide, and fifteen of us had the job of taking care of it. So as not to run out of work, we would botch the job and then start it all over again. One *Blokova* even remarked that before they had a crew of gardeners these little plots had flourished, but now, they were wilting away. With a spade over my shoulder, I could walk around freely all day on the Lagerstrasse, visiting my friends in the different blocks.

Ági was made a *Mistwache*, a garbage guard. No matter how ridiculous it sounds, this was a very important, responsible position. The newly arrived Poles, who had spent four years in the Lodz ghetto, were so starved that they would storm the garbage heaps in order to devour the potato peels and other scraps, and not even cudgel blows would deter them.

That's what had become of man – thanks to Hitler. It was terrible to see this starved, ragged, barefoot crowd. They begged everyone for food and sometimes attacked the food carriers, pushing them aside to get hold of the cauldrons and devour their contents. The *Mistwache*'s job was to keep these people away from the vicinity of the kitchen. Ági carried out this "guard duty" by shouting at anyone trying to approach and by waving her stick around – without doing that she would have been set upon – while she kicked the coveted kohlrabi, cabbage, potato or carrot in their direction.

Around September, we received some new crop potatoes, which was a treat. They were cooked in their peel and served for supper. Even though there was no salt to go with them, by that time our desires were very modest. No one was bothered by the fact that the same grey blankets used to carry them from the kitchen might have been used for carrying corpses the day before. As long as it was food, edible food, the rest didn't matter.

We were getting fresh vegetables and our food had improved. We were even able to eat our meal from "organized" bowls – with spoons. Since it was Ági's job to make sure nobody stole anything, she could organize freely without any worry. Kohlrabis the size of a man's head, splendid carrots and bright red beets ended up on our table, or rather on our bed. We exchanged them with the *Blokova*'s cooks for margarine and honey, putting an end to our starvation once again. What's more, we could even help our friends. At each midday meal call, five to six friends and relatives showed up at our well-laden bed and happily ate our portions, too. The ladies in the pharmacy also received their rations, but since they had better food, they wouldn't eat them and gave them to us as well. We, in turn, passed them on to our friends.

Ági received sweet coffee from the kitchen twice a day, bringing it back triumphantly. She would not drink it alone for the world. In addition, she also got a better quality meal at the kitchen. Our whole group started looking better; we put on weight and colour returned to our cheeks. We began to worry that something bad might happen again, as it always did when things were starting to go well.

In mid-September, the High Holidays arrived. The religious women and girls had been thinking of them ever since our arrival in Auschwitz, consoling each other that by the High Holidays, they would be home again. I had only smiled at this because I predicted that the only way we would survive was if by some miracle the war ended by October. If we were to stay here during the winter, we were doomed. In fact, come October, the most horrific selections started – the culling of the weak.

On the eve of the Jewish New Year, a table covered with a white tablecloth was set up in the centre of the block, with two lit candles on it. Gabi, the *Blokova*, wished everyone a Happy New Year and also that everyone would be celebrating it in her own home next year. This gave rise to such hysterical sobbing, praying and wailing that it took hours to calm down. Anything that wasn't part of our everyday problems, anything that touched our souls, was unbearable. We needed to not think, not feel, or else we'd go crazy.

It was going on five months since we had said goodbye to our loved ones. I had received my husband's farewell letter months earlier and I hadn't heard anything about him or about my one and only dear son since. I took some comfort in the fact that at least they were together. We thanked God every day that Ági had stayed with me and János with his father, which was considered an exceptional piece of luck there. Nor had we heard about Ági's Pali or Zsófi's husband. Ági never talked about how much she suffered from this, but I could tell. She must have felt awful to know that Pali had ended up in Auschwitz because of her. It was eating away at her.

~

In Block 14 we had very pleasant roommates. Acquaintances from Szatmár shared our bunk, as well as a sweet, darling little woman from Gyulafehérvár, Herta Bürger, the wife of Dr. Nemes. She didn't have anybody and was drawn to us, clinging to me as if she were my own daughter. We shared every morsel with each other. I remember one time that Herta triumphantly arrived with a clove of garlic. There is no Parisian perfume whose scent we would have found more enchanting, and for days we rubbed a little bit on our bread to make the enjoyment last for a long time.

At the onset of the cold fall weather, when Ági needed a new pair of shoes, Herta gave up her bread ration for two days so that we could buy boots, which cost two and a half loaves of bread and half a litre of honey. Now that Ági had her pair of shoes and Zsófi had a sweater and trousers, we were not as scared of the winter. But how was Ági to wear the size forty-two men's boots without stockings? That's when we got a very welcome message from my niece Kató. I had been so worried that she had been taken to do hard labour but she was well, together with her governess, and working in the neighbouring Lager, in the clothing warehouse near the crematorium. The message said that she would love to see us.

With Ilonka's help, I managed to get in with the group who went over to the warehouse to get clean clothes for the people in the infirmary. Kató was so happy to see me. From a sweet little dumpling, she had turned into a tall, lanky girl. Her work consisted of sorting the clothes of the victims of the gas chambers. She saw tens of thousands enter the place from which no one ever returned, constantly hearing their cries of agony. The bloom had faded from her cheeks, the child-like, joyful, carefree expression had disappeared from her eyes. At the age of fourteen, she was a mature woman struggling to survive.

At the beginning of October, she bore witness to the revolt staged by the condemned workers tending the crematorium. It was the practice that those who had worked there for three months or so would themselves be incinerated, most likely to leave no eyewitnesses behind. I saw a letter once, sent by a *Sonderkommando*, a crematorium worker, to his wife, who had almost gone mad after reading it. "Fate is catching up with me," he wrote, "the same fate that I have inflicted on others unwillingly! I'm going to die and that is how it has to be. I cannot live on after having incinerated my own parents." He was saying goodbye and at the end of the letter he added, "you will find out when fate catches up with us because we are not leaving without making our mark...."

On that very evening, October 7, 1944, a huge explosion shook the Lager. Women prisoners working in the munitions factory of Auschwitz had gotten hold of explosives, and the *Sonderkommando* workers blew up one of the crematoria. Kató recounted how a naked man ran out of there, screaming, and the workers caught him and pushed him into the fire. He was a German political prisoner and had betrayed them. The few hundred mutineers were killed by a firing squad, but indeed they didn't leave without making their mark – there was one less death chamber.

While Kató was telling me this story, she took off her sweater, her stockings and her kerchief for me, and also gave me a handkerchief. I hid all this in my bosom, and we agreed that I would come back the following Monday, by which time she would have a lot of warm clothes ready for us. I embraced the poor dear and my heart almost broke when I thought about how her mother would feel to see her one and only daughter in such a state. Unfortunately, I knew that her mother would never see her again. Luckily, by her side was her selfless, devoted governess, so at least she wasn't totally alone.

Let winter come; we were going to be well equipped with winter clothing and would not be cold. But Auschwitz wouldn't have been Auschwitz if it had been possible to make plans there, or to be able to count on anything. The discipline had grown so severe that we were not allowed to leave the blocks at all, not even to go to the WC. We had to get used to going to the WC when the *Stubendienst* felt the need, not when we did. We were allowed to go only three times a day, in groups, along with our leaders. Anyone who has never gone through this has no idea how much suffering it can cause. To make matters worse, everyone had a bladder infection or diarrhea.

As the weather turned colder, terrible weeks followed. "Disinfecting," which we all dreaded, was a daily occurrence. The process would start in one block, go through all thirty-two, and then start all over again. On and on. Before almost every disinfection, Ági and I managed to skip out by spending the day in another block with our friends. Disinfecting began around two in the morning; we'd be woken up and the block would be locked to prevent anyone from escaping. Nothing was to be left in the blocks except for the empty bunk beds. The *Stubendienst* did not have to take part because they had to clean the block, collecting all the blankets to be disinfected. Mind you, this meant that everyone got back someone else's blanket instead of her own. If we suspected that it was our turn, we carried our better clothes over to another block. Everyone was trying to keep their worst piece of clothing on because they would never see those clothes again, except on somebody else.

Sometimes we were taken to a completely different Lager for disinfection. The same humiliations that we had been subjected to for the first time on our arrival at Auschwitz started all over again. Stripped naked, shivering in the icy *Waschräume*, sometimes for hours, before it was our turn to be disinfected. In the meantime, our clothes were also disinfected, which really meant disintegration. Then we underwent another round of depilation, except that our hair would not be shorn unless we were found to have lice. The lice, after every disinfection, seemed to multiply with glee. Those who did not have lice before disinfection would definitely have them after. This dreadful procedure served absolutely no purpose but to torment us.

When finally, after a few minutes of showering, we got out of there, a German soldier – one of the ones who had been watching us, snickering – redistributed the clothes, whatever happened to be in hand. Short women got dresses reaching to the ground, tall women ones reaching to the navel, and most of them in shreds. Still, whoever got anything was glad because each time at least a hundred women remained without any clothes at all. There were simply no clothes left.

They would then run naked to the block and wrap a blanket around their chilled bodies. Sometimes it was weeks before someone took pity on them and brought them some sub-standard stuff from the warehouses, where hundreds of thousands of good items of clothing were gathering dust. One of my friends from Szatmár wore a long cotton shirt for weeks, originally white in colour but now turned brown; it made me sick to see her that way. In the cold October rain and wind, half-naked, we ran to our block. There, however, the disinfection was not yet finished. We were made to stand in front of the block, sometimes until the evening, blue from cold, shivering and hungry.

Selections were ongoing in the Lager; however, until now it had always been the strong who were picked for labour transport and the weak who were left behind. Increasingly, there were more weak ones and fewer strong ones in the Lager. This was not an encouraging phenomenon, as we had witnessed what happened to the Czechs once all the strong young people who were fit to work were taken away and only the weak were left, condemned to death. We were haunted by visions of being dragged to the gas chambers in the middle of the night the way they had been.

Our only hope lay in the frequently repeated claim that Block 14 would not undergo selection because it was the block full of strong workers. One time, though, it wasn't the strong ones who were separated out, but the weak ones. It is impossible to imagine what those emaciated children and the more feeble elderly people must have felt: living in constant fear, wondering, every day, whether Mengele would pick them with a jovial smile. Mengele always had a smile on his face – he was at his most cheerful when he was sending the greatest number of people to their death – all the while whistling the *Blue Danube*.

Those selected were put in an empty block. They wouldn't get anything to eat for a day or two, and then one night during a strict *Blocksperre* they would be taken away. The crematoria stuck out their crimson tongues of flame, perhaps to mock God for condoning it. The awful smell turned our stomachs and the awful fear tore at our hearts.

If those who were worried about being grouped with the weak got wind of a new selection, they hid in some other block and only ventured out once the danger had passed. Ági and the other young women who were together with their mothers were sick with worry. After a selection, they came to me one by one, crying on my bosom and lamenting, "My mom was taken away! I wish I could be killed along with her."

At the beginning of October, three of my friends had been taken away in one day, among them the woman who had urged us to go home when the Germans marched into Budapest. Her twenty-three-year-old daughter, together with her two-week-old baby, had been sent straight to the gas chamber on arrival. Her husband, along with their son-in-law, I have just learned, were hit by a bomb. The whole family, along with so many other families, perished completely.

It is impossible to imagine the constant state of anguish in which we lived. My bunkmates were forever pestering me with their questions: "Don't I look like a Muselmann?" [A prisoner near death] "Don't I look too gaunt?" "Won't they make me go up in smoke?" They kept rouging their cheeks with beets to have a healthy look, though, in effect, none of us was in such bad physical shape because we all had "positions" and we were not starving. The whole of Block 14 could have qualified for a labour transport. There were very few older people among us, yet Mrs. Mihály Földi, the wife of the well-known Hungarian author, and Ili Karácsonyi, the famous prima donna, who was in good physical shape because she used to sing for the *Lagerälteste* who was helping her, ended up grouped with the weak.

Ági didn't have a peaceful moment on account of me. It was her *idée fixe* that a selection would occur while she was working near the kitchen and we'd be separated. I tried to laugh it off, as I had lost only about twenty pounds and was still plump – I suited Mengele's taste. To calm her fears, we agreed that if I found out a selection was about to take place in the block, I would flee to Block 9, where our friends from the *Stubendienst* would hide me. Ági left for work with greater peace of mind.

On October 10, the afternoon of the day we had come to this agreement, I was resting without a care when I noticed, to my horror, that the doors were being locked up. I jumped down off the *Koje* as quick as a rabbit and barely managed to sneak out the back door. I ran over to Block 9 and climbed onto the top of a *Koje*. If the *Blokova* caught sight of me, it would provoke a terrible row. I was getting comfortable and had just finished taking off my high lace-up shoes, when the *Blokova*, the horrible Editke, rushed in and started shouting, "Everybody out of the block! Blockdurchsuchung!" (Block search!) I knew what that meant. If someone was found hiding during a search, may God have mercy on her.

By the time I finished putting on my shoes there was not a soul left in the block apart from me. As the doorkeeper, whom I knew, let me out through the back door, the *Muselmänner*, the weak ones from our block, were already being brought in through the front door. It was an awful moment. A minute later, even the back door was being guarded by an SS soldier to prevent anyone from leaving. It was truly a matter of mere seconds before I would have been locked in together with the doomed, with no way out.

I had escaped death row, but where could I go? Every one of these selections was conducted under strict *Blocksperre*, and at the door of each block the doorkeepers – representatives of the highest authority in the Lager – held, if not a flaming sword, a cudgel. The doorkeepers, whose principal function was to ensure that the *Blokovas'* trysts were not disturbed, were held in such high regard by them that they lived very well indeed, and therefore treated everyone as meanly and rudely as possible. The only way to get into or out of the block was through their bodies.

If I was found outside they would know right away that I had escaped from the group of the weak and would take me back there. All of a sudden I noticed, not far from me, a few labourers cleaning the drainage ditches, continuously pulling on a wire cable with great force. Without a word, I joined them and started pulling on the cable with the utmost zeal. They had no idea why I happened to be there, but I started giving them instructions – all the while having no clue as to what we were supposed to be doing – and they must have thought that I had been ordered there by the higher-ups.

After a quarter of an hour of pulling cables, the doors were opened and I saw Ági and Zsófi run, sobbing, over to Block 9. They thought I was locked in there. "My Ágika, I'm here!" I shouted. She was crying so hard that I was unable to calm her down. She had found out that I had fled to Number 9 to avoid the selection, but had encountered locked doors guarded by Germans with pistols at the ready. At last, with great difficulty, she managed to calm down. "Luckily that's behind us now," I said. "We should have peace for a while."

I found out that almost everyone my age had been selected, my good friends and the three young women from Sighet who shared our bed. The block was filled with tears; everybody had lost someone. Still, a few other older women also managed to escape. The wife of a lawyer from Ungvár, a weak, elderly woman, had hidden under the bed in the *Blokova*'s room but the *Blokova* hadn't left her room after the selection, and the woman couldn't get out from under the bed. Finally, what will be, will be, she thought, and crawled out, to the great surprise of the *Blokova*. She thought that the *Blokova* would strike her dead, but instead the *Blokova* grabbed her by the waist and started dancing around with her, for being so crafty.

Slowly everything returned to normal, all the fugitives resurfaced, and we were just getting ready for supper, when all of a sudden the whole block was locked again, and Mengele was already inside. "Get undressed completely!" he shouted. We took off our clothes, frightened, even though Ági and I were together this time. I noticed that one of our bunkmates, Mrs. Samu Fischer, was climbing under the *Koje* because she didn't dare to go through the selection process. We, on the other hand, were ready to go.

This time, Mengele came up with a new formula. He stopped at the door and we had to run out of the block in front of him, naked, in the cold autumn evening, over to Number 13 across the way. A lot of people had escaped the afternoon selection, and this was how he was hoping to catch them. I successfully ran past him, with Ági at my heels, across the Lagerstrasse. We ran like crazy and I only dared to look back, with my heart pounding, when I reached the door of Number 13. Ági was by my side, thank God.

I saw the wife of the lawyer from Ungvár, the one who had escaped under the *Blokova's* bed that afternoon, being pulled back by Mengele, who seized her by the neck with the crook of a stick, like a dogcatcher. Her daughter, Vera, was sobbing beside me, half dazed by the sight. A lot of our acquaintances were taken to the gas chamber that time. We, the strong group of women fit for transport, were able to return to our block later on, and my friend Mrs. Samu Fischer, who had been crammed under the bed for hours, dared to emerge.

Soon after, our wishes came true. I was chosen together with Ági, Zsófi, and all of our bunkmates for a transport. We had no inkling what awaited us, but we sensed that we would need friends and were relieved that we were staying together. We had a sweet little friend in Block 19 as well, Magda Schönberger from Nagyvárad, who was in the *Stubendienst* and who had helped us a lot by bringing us cheese, honey, soup, whatever she could. We were happy when we found out that she and her row of five, all very good friends, had all been selected with us.

The next morning we said farewell to Lager C, where we had suffered so much, to Gabi, the *Blokova*, whose bulky build and flowing mane reminded one of a lioness, but who could slap you around like a gendarme sergeant. She was the embodiment of the female ideal in the Lager – women who were considered heavy-set at home and treated with smiling disdain by the slim, chic fashion plates, were gazed at enviously in this place; they were the pretty ones, they were the Lager beauties. They were the ones who obtained positions, for whom the men threw treasures – bread, clothes, sewing supplies – over the fence. Gabi was the personification of this Lager ideal and, disregarding her penchant for beating up people, she was a good-humoured young thing, who said goodbye to us with a few kind words. "Be happy that you are getting away from these gas chambers. If it was up to me, I'd come along with you." As we heard this, we would not have believed that one day we'd look back with longing at Auschwitz, with its crematoria and gas chambers. Yet that is what happened.

Schlesiersee

On October 22, 1944, we started off toward the disinfection building in the neighbouring FKZ [*Frauen-konzentrationslager*, Women's Lager], where the crematorium stood. This is where my niece worked and she had been waiting, in vain, for me to come and pick up the clothes she had readied for us.

We had barely reached the office when the beautiful Éva Citrom from the pharmacy ran over to us. "Ilonka has found out," she whispered to me, "that this is a very bad transport. Come with me and I will arrange for you to stay behind."

I was willing to step aside, but Ági looked at me pleadingly. "Let's not tempt fate, Mommy," she said. "I'm happy that at last we were picked together, and I am going crazy from fear of being separated. I couldn't bear another selection!" Even though Éva was tearfully begging us to stay, we moved on.

In the disinfecting building, we had to hand over all our clothes again, the nice trousers and sweaters that we had starved for so bitterly. Whatever anyone managed to be in possession of, sooner or later it would invariably end up in the Germans' warehouses. It was the greatest folly to starve in order to obtain clothing, yet we were more afraid of freezing than of starving, so we had to procure warm clothing nonetheless.

This time, however, exceeding our expectations, we were given decent clothing to wear. I ended up with a pair of ruffled white linen pants that went to my ankles, which I implored the girl handing out clothing to exchange for a warm undershirt, slip, dress, sweater and coat. We even got a nightgown, which was a men's pyjama top made longer by the addition of a piece of white linen, but a nightgown none-theless. And stockings! It was the first time in five months that we had stockings on our legs. We had to tie them up with string as they were constantly slipping down, but it made us all the more proud to pull them back up – let everyone see our stockings!

After a hot shower, combing our hair and dressing decently from head to toe, we thought we were in heaven. We received provisions for the trip, two portions of bread, a double ration of salami, and margarine. Imagine our joy when we boarded proper passenger cars instead of cattle cars. We had already forgotten that such things ex-isted, and we started to feel like human beings again and not pariahs – for the last time in a long while.

The accompanying soldiers spoke civilly to us and allowed us to open the windows and walk in the corridors; they even offered us coffee. Somehow, all this lulled us into believing in a brighter future. After the barren Lager where, apart from the sparse blades of grass I was tending, there was no greenery to be seen, the yellowish fields and the flaming forests in their autumn splendour made a sensational impact on us. Where we were heading was, of course, kept secret.

All of a sudden, we arrived at a city. It was well lit and we could see the streets from the station. My God, how this made me feel! Never before had I experienced such bitter heartache. Was it true that there were still people with a life? Elegantly dressed women, babies with smiling faces. We hadn't seen children in five months. During those five months, our minds had dulled – perhaps we didn't even have souls anymore. All that interested us was not to starve and not to be so cold.

From the train, I could see through a window into a house. The gentle light of a lamp fell on a table covered with a white cloth, a family seated around it. A father, mother and four children were having dinner. No, this was impossible to bear, too much of an ordeal for us who had not sat on a chair in five months, who instead had to crouch, backs bent, to avoid hitting our heads on the bunk above. We thought of our old homes only as if they were part of a beautiful dream, from which we would awaken to the harsh reality. I sensed that we would never see our loved ones again; I didn't know where to locate them in my thoughts. My weak, tall, lanky son, János, who lived only for his books. My dear husband, who shared my very thoughts. Where could they be living, if they were living at all?

The tears were streaking down my face as I closed the train curtains, and the optimism that had filled us at our departure evaporated as the train pulled away. We were like falling leaves in the current of the autumn wind…. A miserable night passed and toward dawn, while it was still dark, we arrived at our unknown destination in the pouring rain. As we got out of the carriages, I saw an undulating, menacing body of dark water in front of us. There was water wherever I looked and water streaming down our necks. At last we could decipher the name of the station: Schlesiersee. This was the name of the lake and also of the small town situated on its shore.

Rows of five and marching. The outlines of a pretty little town became visible in the grey, pre-dawn light. Mansions, each one more beautiful than the last, and tidy streets. Not a soul to be seen at this early hour, but behind a few windows a woman's hand would pull aside a snow-white curtain, so suggestive of a peaceful home, and a pair of curious eyes would peer out. I wonder what they felt, what they were thinking, as they caught sight of two thousand women marching in a downpour.

We marched for hours. We left the town behind us and all we saw around us were barren fields. Not a factory chimney in sight, even though it had been our hope to work in a factory. After all, it was almost the end of October – what could we possibly do in the fields? We saw all sorts of windmills, which, previously, I had seen only on

Dutch postcards. My first time seeing a windmill, soon to become the thousand-times-cursed backdrop to the tragedy that would play out on these fields, whose ill-fated protagonists we would become.

We passed through two villages. People who had just gotten up were shaking their heads, watching our sad, drenched company. The rain that had plagued us since the beginning of our exile was still cascading down on us incessantly, trickling down our skin. Our new attire, which we were so proud of, turned into wringing-wet, foul-smelling rags. My stockings, which I had stopped readjusting, slipped down, and I trampled on them; they were in tatters by the time we arrived in front of a small farm that stood all by its lonely self in the fields.

Fear pierced my heart. Could this be the place where we were going to live? In the autumn? In the winter? No! This was unbelievable, surpassing even our most pessimistic imaginings and yet, at the same time, nothing was impossible or unbelievable. We marched into the courtyard of the farm and were made to stand in a quadrangle-shaped formation. Never, not even on my arrival at Auschwitz, had I felt this level of hopelessness. The lack of civilized amenities had been my fear all along. In Auschwitz, I had been reassured by the presence of electricity and *Waschräume*. Now, even the gas chamber seemed better than perishing in this place. From the outset, I was convinced that we would never survive a winter here.

Ági must have been blaming herself for not wanting to stay behind. She looked at me with tears in her eyes, and I could not conceal my own despair. "My Ágika, there we could have died simply, but here we will have to dig each other's grave," I said.

We stood around in the yard for quite a while, in the relentless rain. Then it was announced that we wouldn't all fit in the barn and stable, and a thousand people would have to move on. We were among the ones permitted to stay, but I considered the situation there so terrible that I decided to move on. No matter where they took us, it had to be better than this. We had to risk it.

We had to go another three or four kilometres on rough paths across the fields until we arrived at another farm. From the outside, the building, a huge barn, looked better kept than the other one. In addition, there was a pretty house and a stable. The house was occupied by some sort of an overseer who had a lot of children with red cheeks, blond hair and blue eyes, but a part of the courtyard was separated off for them, lest they should mix with us "cursed" Jews.

We were allowed to choose which would be our next home, the barn or the stable. I chose the barn because I had always been scared of mice and rats and no stable would be without them. We entered our future domicile. The Auschwitz block prisons seemed like royal palaces compared to this place. Here, the only furniture was the straw. Mind you, there was a good thick layer of it covering the floor, and we collapsed on it and went to sleep right away. Given the night journey, the marching and standing around in the rain, it was no wonder we couldn't stand on our feet any longer. We didn't desire anything – nor did we get anything – except to be able to lie down somewhere and stretch our tired, crushed and soaked-to-the-bone bodies. There was no question of having light, or blankets. We huddled together for warmth, and exhaustion rocked us to sleep.

Next day at dawn we heard the fearsome command: "Aufstehen! Aufstehen!" We jumped up, scared, with no idea where we were. *Blokova* arrived and began to drive us out to the yard with their sticks. The rain was still pouring down as we waited to see what was coming. We couldn't even imagine what they might want to do with us. First, thankfully, we were given dishes. In Auschwitz, once we had "organized" a dish of our own we had to hide it, often under our skirts. If the higher-ups noticed this precious treasure, they most certainly would confiscate it, accompanied by a few slaps. We were each given our own red bowl, a mug and a spoon. We wore these tied around our waist with string that we got from the bales of straw.

We had hot coffee that warmed our cold, stiff bodies, and then the *Blokova* announced that today we would be allowed to rest, but that the next day we would have to go into the fields to dig tank traps. We stared at one another, faces pale with fright, eyes desperate and desolate. Many of us had never done any physical labour in our lives back home, and now we were to do the hardest kind of men's work.

That day, we didn't get a meal because the kitchen was not yet set up. We all just lay on the straw, everyone immersed in their thoughts, images conjured up of a horrible, dark future. We were to live in a huge, unheated barn, on straw, just like animals; no WC, only a latrine, which you risked your life to use because you always had to worry about falling into it; and no wash basins, only a pump in the yard. There wasn't electricity either, and we had trampled on each other trying to get to the yard in the dark dawn. We didn't feel like talking.

The next day, our horrid life started. Misery comparable to this was beyond our imaginations. We talked about Auschwitz as we had before about our dear old bourgeois homes. We had stopped thinking about ever sleeping in a bed on white pillows under silk quilts. Instead, we were wondering if we'd ever have a wooden *Koje* made out of fifteen-centimetre boards and nice warm blankets, the way we had it in Auschwitz.

There were some among us who found reassurance in the farm's sole advantage: no crematorium. Ági also belonged to this group, but not I. My only desire was to die as soon as possible, to have it over with. We would not bear this for long, so why suffer? If this place had been surrounded by an electrified wire fence, I don't believe I would have thought twice about grabbing hold of it to end my life. But Ági, Zsófi, Herta, and the rest of the young ones wanted to live, at any cost. To be happy with their young husbands, whose company they had enjoyed for only a few weeks. That's why they tried to adapt to the immutable, and their youthful pliability helped them to not lose heart completely. Their will to live had to overcome the difficulties that were growing more and more horrible by the day. Slowly, their will consoled me too, and later on it was I who encouraged them when their will to live dwindled.

Our daily routine began with a wake-up call at 4:30 a.m. We didn't need to get dressed because we wore our entire wardrobe day and night, with the exception of our coats, which we used as blankets, and our shoes, which according to the tried-and-true recipe, we used as pillows. We put on our shoes and coats in the pitch dark and went to stand outside. Coffee was distributed. The *Lagerführer* appeared. Our *Lagerälteste* was a good-looking Slovak woman in her forties, but her sweet smile concealed a lot of meanness, and the *Blokova* lived up to their leader. The meanest was Eszti, who looked like a madam, followed closely by a half-Aryan Dutch woman, the beautiful Joki. In addition, there were about twenty soldiers guarding us, who accompanied us on the way to work.

The thousand people were divided into ten companies, each one headed by an *Anweiserin*. They had a splendid position; they didn't need to work yet they received double portions of food. Of course, according to the Germans' taste, these leaders were selected from among the biggest, fattest young women. We were assigned to the fourth company. Our *Anweiserin* was a friend from Nagyvárad, Manci Indig, and she selected the leaders who would be in charge of four groups of twenty-five people. We formed a group that was very pleasant and worked together all the time, but the other three groups of twenty-five consisted of ill bred, greedy, aggressive people, and they were always giving us trouble.

We were asked who would like to do housework and, knowing that I would not be able to take the outdoors, given my bad legs, I signed up. I was accepted, and therefore I belonged to the house company, the so-called *Hofkommando*. I managed to stay indoors for a few days but more and more people who belonged to the other companies got sick and stayed in, and they were replaced by members of the house company because there was a strict rule that each company needed at least ninety to march out. Every morning, the physician – a lovely person, Dr. Eta Pickler, a dentist from Budapest – had to report on how many invalids there were. One time, she couldn't answer right away and the *Lagerälteste* slapped her face so hard that my own face reddened. Eta has long since forgiven her, but from that day on I hated this mean beast with her sweet smile.

For a few days, this rule about the number needed to march out caused me a lot of problems. I was removed from the house company and not only did I have to march out, but I was put in a completely strange company, wherever anyone was missing, separated from my friends. I got fed up with the constant worry and finally resigned from the coveted house company of my own volition.

In the cold October dawn, I set out for our bitter work in rows of five with the rest from my company. By the time it grew light we were supposed to be at the field, which meant starting off in the pitch dark, accompanied by the moon and the stars. The countryside was completely barren. Only the continuously revolving blades of the windmills sliced through the air, as if they were grinding our sad days. The wind never stopped for a second, an eternally blowing, accursed wind that chilled us to the bone and became our worst enemy. We had quite a few enemies: the rain, the cold, the blowing snow, the mud and the terrible hunger, but we were most defenceless against the wind. It blew through our light clothing, and the wet garments froze to our skin.

How many times did Ági tell me, "Mum, I never want to see another windmill, not even on a postcard." We marched, hanging on to each other, our teeth chattering, far away, past the first farm that had made such an awful impression on me when we first arrived. It took us at least an hour and a half to arrive at the place where we'd be working.

Little sticks in the field marked the area that we were to dig up. We had to dig trenches, tank traps that were four metres wide and would narrow at the bottom like a coffin, three and a half metres deep, extending for a hundred metres in length. We held the spades so awkwardly that even the leaders had a good laugh when they saw us. Shivering from the numbing cold, we started working, and slowly, as the sun came up, it would turn even colder. We grew to hate the sunrise. During my trips over the sea, or vacationing in the mountains, I often used to ask to be woken up at dawn just to take delight in the sunrise. Now I had the pleasure of enjoying this sight every morning, and we all dreaded it in advance.

In general, all the beauty and wonders of nature lost their effect on us. The moon and the stars were still shining brightly when we were made to stand in the courtyard. Every dawn, we saw them disappear among the clouds, and the rising sun found us at our place of work. In the afternoon, we toiled until the sun set, usually bright red – forecasting wind – and the moon was up again by the time we got back to the farm and dropped down on the rotting straw.

We dug until nine o'clock, making slow progress. Our hands got blistered, but at least the work warmed us up a bit. This was the hardest part of the day.

Then a whistle signalled the time for breakfast. This consisted of two small slices of bread saved from the previous supper and a raw potato if we could get hold of one or found some in the ground while digging. We tried to take very small bites to make it last longer. People who hadn't been able to resist temptation the night before and had consumed their full bread ration watched us enviously. Herta usually brought coffee or tea in a bottle, and for a moment we staved off the gnawing hunger. A quarter of an hour later, another whistle sounded, and we started work again in a better mood.

A person was situated every two metres along the ditch and behind each of them stood two more people, two metres apart. The one in front dug first, throwing the earth behind her, and the one next in line would throw it further, forming little mounds. The last one moved it even further and flattened it down. When we reached the depth of one metre, the farmers from the surrounding area brought horse-drawn ploughs and made the ditch deeper. Then, we climbed into the ditch again and continued throwing and flattening the earth.

As the ditch got deeper, everybody wanted to work inside it to be somewhat protected from the wind. I usually sat on the ladder inside the ditch, not pushing myself, trying to entertain the girls with stories of my memories of better times, of lovely trips and balls. I felt that this helped the work progress, but I found it hard to believe that I had experienced all those things, that I had once lived in a better and more beautiful world. When I looked at my rags, my frozen hands, my red legs with no stockings, it truly seemed incredible.

"Yellow is coming!" someone shouted, and I started shovelling or digging so the supervisor would not catch me "sabotaging." The collective noun "Yellows" comprised the SA soldiers with yellow collar patches who directed our work. They were always beating and striking and yelling.

We worked, chatting, freezing and pushing forward the minutes that moved, very slowly, until dinner. The Dinner! I have to write it with a capital D. This was the much longed for highlight of the day, what we had been waiting for from early morning, with our eyes hollow from hunger, our heads spinning, our stomachs churning. We were constantly watching to see if the two carts bringing the cauldrons were coming. The first person to spot the small black dot approaching from afar would shout triumphantly. Then we had trouble working, waiting for the redeeming whistle to the point that it made our stomachs and hearts quiver.

When, at last, it sounded, we could crawl out of the ditch and wipe off our dusty bowls and even dustier clothes. Everyone liked to be the first to quell their hunger but on the other hand, it was sad to stand there with your empty dish and watch the others receiving their food, still having the heavenly enjoyment ahead of them. Therefore, exercising great will power, we let the people who were elbowing and clawing push ahead of us, waiting patiently at the end of the line for our turn. It's true that sometimes there was no food left for the ones standing at the end, but at least one didn't get punched in the stomach or elbowed in the side by the aggressive women from Máramaros.

Manci was the distributor, and occasionally there was some food left at the bottom of the cauldron. The Máramaros girls swung into action once again, pushing everyone aside and storming the pot, often knocking Manci down, scrambling over one another to scoop out what was left. These crafty and aggressive girls appeared to be in better shape. We were losing weight, getting greyer by the day, while they – who had been used to physical labour, the adversities of weather, and poorer nutrition – were flourishing.

The half litre of potato soup was good, but insufficient to fill us up. At most, our hunger was momentarily stilled. I couldn't think of a thickened potato soup, the kind I was used to back home. This dish consisted of a few cooked, peeled potatoes in a roux made from some strange flour-like preparation that in addition, I believe, to bromide, also contained other unrecognizable ingredients.

A whistle blew to signal the end of the rest period and we crawled back into the ditch. We discussed whether the food distribution had been fair and how many potatoes each of us had gotten, jealous of those who managed to end up with two whole potatoes in their soup. I always ate only the broth and gave the potato to Ági. She, in turn, did not like meat, and if she happened to come across some shreds of horse meat in her soup she would pass them on to me. At times like this, she was proud and happy.

After three weeks of miserable labour, freezing and starving, the first trench was finished. It had the shape of a coffin, and as, day by day, more and more of us got sick and keeled over, I always felt that this was what it would become.

The Infirmary

In the Lager, the sick were treated disgracefully. They lay on straw, covered with blankets, in a part of the barn designated as the infirmary. As I wrote previously, each company had to have at least ninety people for marching out, and the house company needed at least forty people, so we were allowed sixty invalids at most. Illnesses, however, ignored this rule, and after three weeks we had not sixty but 100 to 120 sick people. They were required to report to the doctor in the morning before leaving for work. She examined them, but was under strict orders to admit only those whose fever was above 38 degrees Celsius. Sticks were used to drive out the ones whose fever only reached, say, 37.8. These women would often collapse in the field and be transported back at noon by the meal cart – dead, on more than one occasion.

The infirmary was the most awful place. Sixty to seventy unkempt, unwashed women lying on rotting straw, doing their business in open buckets. There were only two nurses and they often didn't have time to empty them. The stench was ghastly, and if someone arrived with a minor problem, say, the flu, she had to be prepared to pick up a whole range of diseases there. Most invalids had serious abscesses, which would invariably get infected and spread. There were women who spent the whole three months lying there because their abscesses, instead of healing, were continuously spreading. There was only one kind of medication, ichthyol, and everyone was treated with this black ointment.

Doctor Eta was a true human being and a doctor who wanted to heal, and she suffered for this impossibility. Every morning, she would cry along with those whom she had to send out, sick, to do hard labour. She stood up to the *Lagerälteste*, and even the German commanding officers, on behalf of the sick, but in vain. No more than sixty were allowed to stay behind, and among these were some healthy women with pull, who were sewing or knitting for the *Blokovas*. So, if it happened that seventy people had a high fever, the extra people needed to fill the quota were drawn from the house company.

As the days passed and it turned into November, then December, more and more people got sick. Most of us had frostbite on our hands and feet. Everybody was covered with bandages made of paper, while margarine paper was used as a substitute for Billroth batiste, a water-proof dressing. Apart from the cold and starvation, we were dealing with a complete lack of hygiene, which is why we longed for Auschwitz where we could get washed every day (in ice-cold water, under a fau-cet, but washed nevertheless). Here, washing was almost impossible even before the pump in the yard had frozen up. Only those with the most energy – and I belonged to that group – would get up in the middle of the night, between two and three o'clock, to go to the well in the freezing cold for a bucket of water and bring it back to the block, though this was strictly forbidden. We made sure that the night watchman, one of the authority figures in the Lager, did not notice.

Every evening, Ági asked me to wake her up for the night ablutions, but if she didn't wake up at the first quiet call, I didn't have the heart to rouse her. After all, she was so tired and exhausted all the time. On occasions like this, I would wake up Zsófi or another friend and make them happy with the leftover water.

Two weeks later, the well froze up. The less chance we had to wash, the more we were infested by itch mites and, to our disgrace, body lice. The first louse was spotted on an invalid's clothes during an examination in the infirmary. In dismay, Eta called for the *Lagerälteste*. She rushed in and loudly proclaimed that she would never again set foot in the infirmary. After five years of captivity – she was a Czech political prisoner – she did not want to die of typhus. Eta, she said, was free to do whatever she wanted. At this point, Doctor Eta also raised her voice. She declared that in her estimation it was not the life of the *Lagerälteste* that was important, but the lives of the thousand people in her charge, and she should feel ashamed for this selfish and irresponsible talk. We were trembling to see what would happen next. I was afraid that she would attack Eta again, but it seems she was wary of the *Lagerführer*, so she just stomped out angrily.

The lice did not stop at the demarcation line, the border of the infirmary; slowly but surely, they covered us all. You cannot imagine a more horrible feeling than this. On the day we discovered the first louse on our clothes, we killed it with disgust, but the next day thirty new ones were born from the nits. By the third day, their army was innumerable. From that time on, though we were dead tired after work, we had a new occupation: searching for lice. Everybody was busy doing it all the time, jostling near the light of the one and only weak bulb in the otherwise dark barn to carry out this job. Before long, head lice joined their relatives, which was no surprise, as our hair had grown out in the last half year and we didn't have combs, brushes, or the possibility of washing. Finally, one of the girls received a fine-toothed comb as a present from a *Vorarbeiter*, a foreman. She loaned it to us for a slice of bread per head – luckily not per louse.

After the *Lagerälteste*'s first outburst, she simply took the issue of lice off the agenda, kept away from the infirmary, and did not concern herself with the sick and the lice-ridden. These poor souls suffered more and more every day, fearing typhus. However, we didn't need typhus in order to perish. The hunger, the cold, the rotting straw, the inhuman treatment by the Germans, the unscrupulousness of our leaders, all did the job without an epidemic. For it was the obvious goal of the Germans to make as many people die as possible.

In the meantime, there were certain measures that seemed to protect our health. One evening, after having returned from our bitter labours, when we could hardly stand on our feet, we were not allowed to enter the barn. We had to undress outside and were only allowed to enter one by one. Then, we were inoculated against typhus by a German doctor and an army of nurses clad in brilliant white who had come from the neighbouring towns. This was carried out under absolutely sterile conditions, the needle disinfected after each injection. Again we had to see that our miserable existence, living like animals, wasn't the norm and that culture, cleanliness, well-groomed women and smiling faces still existed. Our hearts ached. We were better off forgetting about these things, just to be able to keep living.

The inoculation process was repeated three times over three weeks. The fact that we had to lie down on rotting straw with our sterilized injection site, that we weren't able to wash, that we were infested by lice, that we were driven out to work in spite of the high fever caused by the inoculation – was none of their concern.

~

We carried on with our horrible drudgery, day after day, even on Sundays, in the rain, snow and mud. According to a rule, if it was raining at the time of departure, we didn't have to march out, but this occurred only once or twice. What regularly occurred was that it had been pouring all night, as reported happily by those returning from the latrine, but by the time we needed to leave, the rain had stopped. It was as if the weather conspired against us.

One time, after a terrible rainy November night, the weather cleared up by morning and we marched out. Awful wooden clogs, which were given to people when their shoes had worn out, got stuck in the mud at each step, and required a complicated manoeuvre to pull out. Someone always slipped and ended up in a puddle. After the long, slippery, exhausting trek, we finally arrived at our work site. We stopped at the edge of the deep ditch and were horrified to see that it was filled with water up to our knees. "We don't have to crawl in there, do we?" we asked the leader, hopefully. "Of course you do!" she responded. "Let's go, into the ditch, and bail out the water, quickly."

At this point, as if on command, we all started wailing. It was impossible to bear. I sat down on a big rock, crying bitterly, maybe for the first time since we had left Auschwitz. When Ági saw me crying, she began sobbing even harder. There was nothing we could do; we were forced to get into the ditch. We climbed down the ladder into the hole and, amidst sobs, bailed the water, most of which, of course, like a curse, landed back on our heads.

By this time, the wind launched its onslaught. The wet clothes froze to our skin, the countless wounds on our hands and legs hurt like crazy from the cold. We dug and bailed until the sun went down. At last the whistle blew to end work, and we dragged ourselves miserably back along the slippery, now frozen road. Had we been asked which part of us hurt, we wouldn't have been able to answer. We were hurting body and soul alike.

When we arrived after a whole day of bitter work, frozen to the bone, we were not allowed to enter the barn to take a rest. The *Blokova* never made it that easy for us. Sometimes we had to wait for hours at the entrance to the Lager before it was our turn to enter, since supper was distributed at the door. There were cauldrons filled with flour soup or, on rare occasions, with potatoes cooked in their skins. The *Blokova* standing there would push a slice of bread into our hands and whatever else was our due. What joy it was when, one time, we got a spoonful of sugar to go with the bread, and when we were given marmalade or some sort of artificial honey, it was a red-letter day. The soup consisted of some bitter flour mixed with water; if it was salted, we ate it, but sometimes there was no salt in the Lager for weeks on end. With starvation at hand, we could only swallow the tasteless but hot – and therefore longed-for – liquid with disgust.

December arrived, bringing with it severe cold that led to further suffering. We were cold at dawn, standing in the yard with shivering limbs; we were cold on the march; we were cold out in the field; and we were cold in the evening in the barn. A gigantic stove, a monstrosity almost reaching the ceiling, was set up, but it was impossible to heat a wooden barn with a roof full of cracks. In addition, none of the doors closed properly, and since, all night long, the women suffering from bladder infections and diarrhea made trips to and from the latrine, the stove ended up heating the yard. The stove was good for one thing, though. After a rainy day, we could dry our soaked clothes beside it. On those days, after having returned from hard labour, going to bed was out of the question. We stood almost all night, jostling one another for a place near the stove, drying the clothes on our bodies to avoid having to leave in wet clothes the next day, in the cold dawn. Of course, I didn't let Ági stay up at night. I was the one who dried her wet clothes, spending the whole night beside the stove, at times so sleepy that I would fall onto it.

Then, the news spread that we would be getting warm clothes! Our joy and excitement knew no bounds. Further weeks passed in expectation and, at last, a clothes shipment did indeed arrive from Auschwitz. The clothes were taken first to the number one farm where the *Oberscharführer* lived. He was an awful man. On the few times that he came to inspect our place, we shook with fear. Once, he noticed that the wife of a doctor, Dr. István Schwarcz from Szatmár, had stuffed her coat with straw and he personally struck her twenty-five times. It was such bad luck that he spotted her, since all of us were constantly stuffing our coats with straw to make the terrible cold more bearable. In this way, slowly, all of our "furnishings," the bed linen and furniture for which the straw was a substitute, wandered off to the fields. After this incident, we were inspected every morning, so we no longer dared to use the stuffing. Of course, that meant we were feeling the cold even more while waiting for the promised warm clothes.

This *Oberscharführer* was terribly harsh and strict – and scary looking, with a death's head symbol on his hat – yet those staying at his farm had a better lot than we did. So, all things considered, we got the short end of the stick for not having stayed at the first farm. A few women from the first farm kept coming to see Dr. Eta to have their teeth cared for, and they all seemed to be in fine shape, dressed in good, warm clothes after the clothing distribution. Whereas over at our place everyone was stealing, they told us that nobody stole over there, that their soldiers weren't sending home heavy food parcels every day like ours were. Even though Death's Head beat them for the slightest infraction, he made sure that they all received what was their due. Their people had much better meals, we could tell. They didn't look as pitiful as we did, we who were wasting away and getting greyer by the day.

The first farm selected the best of the clothes shipment and sent us what was left. Dresses, coats and sweaters for two thousand had been sent from Auschwitz, so everyone should have received one of each, but that's not what happened. The lucky ones managed to get something, the unlucky ones almost nothing. The German women and the *Blokova* had dresses made from the undistributed clothes and had sweaters unravelled so socks, gloves and pullovers could be knit for themselves. As we looked worse and were dressed worse, our leaders became fatter and better dressed.

Ági and I were relatively lucky. We each got a skirt and a spring coat, and Ági even got a sweater. We chopped off the bottom of the old quilted coat until it became something like a spencer, a short, close-fitting jacket and, combining the bottom part with the skirt, we had a pair of pants, some headwear and gloves sewn for us. Who cared if one leg of the pants was blue and the other grey! We no longer noticed such trifles. It was a much bigger problem that we had to give up our bread in exchange because the seamstresses were working outdoors as well during the day, and they would make us pay handsomely for having to spend their nights sewing. We gave up our bread nonetheless, more afraid of the cold than the starvation, which we had become accustomed to. We were always dizzy and it wasn't so much hunger we felt but, rather, an infinite weakness.

Now that we were more warmly dressed, our bleak morning mood lightened as well. Sometimes I started singing to cheer up the company, and gradually they would all sing along with me. There were two hit songs popular back home then, trite, kitschy tunes, but they suited our situation so well that we kept repeating them: "The world lasts for but a day" and "You are fleeing, you are running in vain – there is no way you can run away from your fate!" A song would start out joyfully and finish drowned in tears.

At other times, we entertained ourselves with "cooking." This was a favourite sport of ours. Everyone related what she would cook and eat "if we go home." These were the visions of our empty stomachs – pipe dreams. One of our workmates put together such sumptuous menus that they made our mouths water. She was wallowing in whipped cream and chocolate to the point that even listening to it gave us indigestion, considering our shrivelled-up stomachs.

Somehow, this made the miserable day pass. When it was getting close to four o'clock no one was able to work any more, but that is when the horrific "Yellows" usually showed up and we would frantically start to work again. They decided the amount and pace of work and, like slave drivers, were always on our backs to check if we were sabotaging. Our work leader happened to be a decent old man – a harmless shoemaker – who would have much preferred to be at home, beside his last, working for his family instead of ordering around weak, sick women. He didn't take his job too seriously but he would shout that much louder whenever he saw an SA officer approaching. "Jön a sárga!" (Yellow is coming!), he would shout in Hungarian – he had heard this battle cry from us so many times that even he learned it – and then we'd start working at top speed.

One time, a Yellow noticed that our excellent *Anweiserin*, Manci, had hidden the ones who were ailing in a huge tool chest, to spare them from having to work. This caused a lot of trouble. The Yellow pulled the women out of the box, where they had been crouching miserably all day, and beat them soundly. He fired Manci and chose Bella, a fat, red-cheeked girl from Nagyvárad, to replace her. With her, there was no longer any order in our company. Manci, who had even been a supervisor back home, was good-hearted and smart, well regarded by everyone, and she maintained discipline. Although Bella, young and inexperienced, was a hard worker, she didn't know how to make others work and nobody heeded her orders. Yet, the Yellow brought her a bun with ham every day. There was no longer order at mealtime and the aggressive women from Máramaros welcomed the slackening of discipline. More than once, no food was left for the people at the end of the line. What this meant – I don't need to describe.

Manci reported her firing to the *Lagerälteste*, who, knowing her worth, appointed her to be head of the *Hofkommando*. She was demoted upward. She no longer had to march out and would be in charge of housework instead. She had to work an awful lot, beginning with sweeping the yard and ending with burials, but she filled this position extremely well, too.

The bitter days kept passing. The wetness made the shoes rot off my feet. My two little bare toes peeked out through the gaping holes and both got frostbitten. Ági's feet had been frostbitten for a long time. She asked for a pair of Dutch wooden shoes – *Klompen* – and she gave me her boots, the ones we had procured at Auschwitz at the cost of great privation. You see, her feet were not cold in the wooden shoes because she got enough foot cloths to go with them, except they were extremely hard to lift; I couldn't take one step in them. Ági, however, happily reported that her feet were not cold at all during work.

In contrast, I suffered terribly in the rock-hard men's size forty-two boots with no stockings. In Auschwitz, I always used to say that I would stay alive only as long as my shoes from home lasted. They protected my poor feet, plagued by rheumatism, sciatica and arthritis. As soon as they were gone and I put on the heavy boots, disaster struck – blistered heels, open wounds that hurt like crazy, and little toes that swelled up to three times their size and turned black from frostbite. For weeks, I was limping in anguish. The foreman didn't mind my not doing any work, but if you stood around in the cold without working, you'd freeze to death. The cart transporting our meal often had to carry back women who'd frozen to death, usually those who'd been forced out despite being sick.

Thus, in spite of all my pains, I kept shovelling. By the evening, on our way back, I couldn't stand on my feet. The children practically dragged me, holding on to my arms. Once I got back, I lay down on the straw, unable to eat. As my feet warmed up, the pain inflicted by the frostbite kept increasing. It was agony. I would have liked to scream, but I didn't want to aggrieve Ági further, so I suffered in silent desperation. It took a few hours before my pains subsided and I managed, with great difficulty, to fall asleep.

One morning, however, my feet were in such a state that I could not put my shoes on at all. Barefoot, carrying my boots in my hand, I reported to the doctor, risking and fearing that I could be sent out to the field like that, which had happened to others. Dr. Eta declared that she couldn't admit me with such minor wounds. Ági and Zsófi cried even more loudly than I did, and my face must have reflected such despair that Dr. Eta took pity on me. She admitted me to the infirmary and sent out in my place a seamstress who was just feigning illness.

I stayed in the infirmary for days, waging my battle against lice, chatting with Dr. Eta while she was dressing my wounds. During one conversation, we realized that we were distant relatives. From that moment on, Eta became our benefactor the same way Ilonka, the pharmacist, had been in Lager C.

It was thanks to her that my fate and that of my loved ones took a turn for the better. Namely, she found a place for me in the *Schälküche*, the potato-peeling kitchen. No more than sixteen people were allowed to work in this kitchen, and seven of them had pull and were placed there by the *Lageralteste*. They worked there all the time, and another nine were selected from the group of women in the infirmary who were no longer sick but were still not capable of marching out. I managed to get to this paradise, which was a much-envied, wonderful position. My age should have entitled me to it, not to mention the fact that I couldn't even put my shoes on, but these things counted for nothing in that place.

The *Schälküche*

The *Schälküche* deserves a separate chapter. Its setting was a coach house-like chamber – windowless, dim, airless, a dirt floor. It was outfitted with a small flat-topped stove and a few wooden planks placed on top of two empty buckets, where the potato peelers sat. To sit! To sit in a warm place! I'm trying, perhaps in vain, to make you understand what this meant. Anyone who doesn't know what it means to hack, dig and shovel in a frozen field, to get soaked and chilled right through without any chance to sit down, cannot imagine what happiness it was to sit peeling potatoes in a warm place.

I had to be there at three thirty in the morning, when the others still had two more hours of sleep. We peeled from four in the morning until the companies marched out. With the onset of the severe cold weather, the workers were roused at five thirty and sent on their way at six thirty, still in the pitch dark, nevertheless. The night watchman would shake me and I would carefully disentangle myself from Ági's embrace – she always snuggled up to me in her sleep – so as not to awaken her. I kissed her gently, got dressed and set out to deal with the precious treasure, the potato. It was always kept under lock and key, and we had to wait in the yard for a German soldier to open the door. Then we entered the icy, unventilated chamber, cleaned it and swept the previous day's peels into the corner for the German farmers who had brought the potatoes to take back for the pigs.

Two women quickly left to fetch the coal that we officially received, but our stove operated on coke, which, on the other hand, you could only "organize," steal, from the storeroom of the Germans' kitchen. This was a rather risky enterprise, causing a great deal of anxiety every day, and only experienced organizers could undertake it. One of us ran to fetch embers from the infirmary, which was heated all night, and another was an expert at preparing and lighting the fire.

The soldier locked the door behind us, lest we hand out potatoes to anyone, and we began selecting out the large potatoes. The small ones were cooked in their skins and served once a week as our long-awaited dinner. Our fingers, numb from the winter's night, were only able to work after being warmed by the fire, burning with crackling flames. My God, what a sorry state my hands were in. From all that peeling I could no longer straighten my fingers; every morning my cramped fingers were in excruciating pain before being fit to peel again. Dirt was engrained in my hands to the point that I thought that it would never fade away in this life. Yet, just sitting beside the warm stove and peeling, my happiness was indescribable. Everyone sought out like-minded people, chatting quietly.

Our *Anweiserin* was a young, pretty little Czech woman who took her job extremely seriously. You were allowed to steal as long as she did not notice it, and we all used potatoes as our currency. The *Anweiserin* had dresses and anything else she needed sewn for herself in exchange for raw or cooked potatoes. She spent all day cooking for her Czech friends who had to march out, so they could have a warm meal waiting in the evening. I had trouble getting a chance to do too much of my own cooking, but in the morning I was always able to cook a small mugful of potatoes for Ági. Sometimes I was able to cook for myself during the day, so I saved my Lager soup for the children. Oh, the joy with which they received that cold, awful soup! How many kisses I got for it!

I found a very interesting group of people in the *Schälküche*, but a rather grim atmosphere. The *Anweiserin* had two Czech friends in the peeling kitchen, very unpleasant women who didn't work at all, and we had to do their jobs as well. We had three "fainters." These young women had been in the infirmary but could not remain there any longer. They couldn't march out either, because their dizziness would have caused them to tumble into the ditch.

A beautiful, presentable girl from Kolozsvár collapsed three or four times a day, like a sack. It was awful to watch. She always fell backwards and we had to make sure that there was nothing behind her that she could hurt her head on. It took her a very long time to come to and we often needed to call the doctor to revive her. She had never had any problems back home.

Fainter number two was a gorgeous girl from Csepel called Anci, who was not even sixteen. She had bright black eyes, red cheeks and curly, coal-black hair. She looked scary when she fainted because instead of turning pale, her face became even redder. She was fond of fainting right on top of me, which she did several times a day, but she also liked to stand or sit beside the glowing red stove, and I had to engage in hand-to-hand combat to move her away from there. I was sick with worry, so afraid that she would fall on the stove and burn her beautiful little face. My heart ached for her.

The third one, Veronka, was a funny fainter, an out-and-out hysterical girl from the country. She fainted then and there and for as long as was necessary. She was roly-poly with a pretty face, and the way she conducted her affairs, she would have made a good politician. Whenever some harder work needed to be done, Veronka would right away declare, with the face of a martyr, that she'd take it. She would start the work, but in a few minutes she would faint dead away. However, she had an amazing knack for choosing the location for her fainting spell, and thus she never hurt herself, while the other two girls were always covered in purple and blue bruises. She told us the most mindless stories, in which she was always the protagonist. We were bored by them, but she wasn't.

Setting the fire was the specialty of a woman named Bella, and she was as proud of it – shall we say – as a church builder would be of his masterpiece. She was very good at sweeping and she took pride in this as well, but she was proudest of all of her sister, who worked in the Germans' kitchen and thus was very powerful, at least as far as organizing went.

Our peeling kitchen also had a prima donna, a soubrette and a comedian, except they were not aware of it. I was richly entertained in this set-up, together with the two friends I made there. They were both from Érsekújvár, pleasant, intelligent women who helped pass the time agreeably during these seemingly endless days. We chatted quietly about our past life, our trips, our families, and about the future, which promised to be very dark. We saw no hope of ever getting out alive from the clutches of the Germans.

As we conversed, we roasted potatoes for ourselves. This was a big deal because previously I, along with those who were marching out, had eaten potatoes raw if we could get hold of them. In the peeling kitchen we cut thin slices, salted them, put them on top of our bread, which was spread with margarine, and ate them heartily. They tasted good and most of all they filled our stomachs. All our acquaintances were begging for potatoes. I would have liked nothing better than to distribute the entire contents of the storeroom, but it was awfully difficult to steal that many potatoes.

Once we had filled all three cauldrons in the kitchen, we stole the potatoes, not from our peoples' rations but from the Germans – for our people – and this was a great thrill. It was the *Anweiserin*'s job to guard the Germans' potatoes, so we were always at risk of being caught, which would have meant being dismissed from the peeling kitchen. Therefore, although everyone was organizing, from the *Anweiserin* on down, it was dangerous and had to be carried out so that no one would notice.

I carefully made hidden pockets in my coat to stow the loot. In spite of the locked door, we managed to find a way to sneak potatoes out to our families. We dug an opening at the bottom of the door that was large enough to allow a dish to be pushed through. In order to fill the stomachs of my immediate family, our row of five, I had to hand out fifty potatoes every day. Only after having eaten ten roasted potatoes did they feel that their stomachs were full. A woman from Máramaros undertook the task of roasting, in ashes, the fifty potatoes at night and got ten of them in payment. When the potatoes were ready she woke the children, who feasted on them happily and went back to sleep, and most likely their dreams were more pleasant than they would have been on an empty stomach.

Our friend Magda, who had helped us so much in Auschwitz, was there too, with her family. They also needed fifty potatoes per day to save them from starvation. I rarely succeeded in sneaking out this extra quantity. Then there was the wider circle of friends from Szatmár. As the starvation reached unbearable levels, everyone was begging for potatoes. Women were even risking their lives for a turnip here and there, left in the ground by the farmers until late autumn. If the soldiers guarding them noticed that someone ventured into the turnip field, they would shoot.

When I entered the peeling place, I put a tiny, four-decilitre mug – we all had one – on the stove to cook the potato in, stirring in a little margarine and salt as well, which I got in exchange for a potato. Everyone had family among those marching out and did the same. Sixteen little mugs huddled together on top of the red, glowing stove. In the meantime, if we could find a spot, we stuck thick slices of potato on the side of the stove to roast. If I was able to prepare a slice for Ági, I was happy.

We always heard the sudden shout from the Lager· "Wake up! Wake up! Get up fast!" Within moments, the barn resembled a busy beehive. The girls were waking up, dressing quickly because those who didn't move fast enough were hastened by the *Blokovas'* sticks. Ági came over to the locked door and quietly called, "Mum!" What sweet music this was for me every morning, as we hardly had a chance to talk. When I left in the small hours, she was still sleeping like a baby, so I just kissed her and pulled the covers up, and didn't see her until they came back.

I always jumped up in haste and, casting frightened glances at the *Anweiserin*, who pretended not to notice, gave Ági the hot food through the opening. She was grateful for this little bit of extra food. Though it would have made more of a difference had she eaten it by herself, she couldn't not share every bite with Zsófi. That wouldn't have been my Ági. Each of them ended up with just a few spoonfuls but at least they didn't leave for work on an empty stomach. If I managed to give them hot potato slices as well, they put them in their pockets and nibbled on them slowly, all the while warming their frozen hands with them. They also pushed their blankets through the opening, thanking me a thousand times for the food, and then set out on their miserable day. Ági always reassured me that the weather was not too bad, that it was going to be a rather pleasant day.

Ági passed the family blankets in through the hole so they would have something warm to cover themselves with when they arrived home frozen in the evening. The blankets had become a serious problem. On the day after our arrival, everybody was given a brand new, warm, grey blanket finished with thread around the edges. Thread was a priceless treasure, and everybody undid the stitches right away. These blankets were collected every morning and handed out in the evening, but somehow by evening there were, say, only nine hundred left of the thousand. Day by day, the blankets diminished in number. Finally, there remained only one blanket for every five people, and in December, in the cold barn, everyone nearly froze to death.

The missing blankets had been turned into underwear, stocking substitutes, gloves; otherwise it would have been impossible to endure working in the cold. When the Germans caught on to this, they carried out blanket inspections. No one was allowed to enter the barn without being inspected to see if she was wearing pieces of clothing made out of blankets, and woe to those who were found out. They didn't get supper, not even bread, were soundly beaten and forced to stand out in the yard all night long.

After the workers had left and the Lager quieted down, the *Lagerführer*, *Aufseherin*, and *Lagerälteste* strode in to count us to see if we were all there. Since we couldn't crawl out through the keyhole… miraculously, we were. Because we were locked up while the companies marched out, we were not subject to the risk of being suddenly assigned to work in the fields, unlike all the other Lager inhabitants, even the *Stubendienst*. This was one of the many advantages to this coveted position, but we certainly worked for it.

As soon as the door opened, we rushed into the sanctuary of the kitchen, where sometimes, if we were lucky, we were given leftover tea for washing the potatoes. Otherwise we would have to wash them in the icy well water. Here they put washed, peeled potatoes in the soup, unlike in Auschwitz, where we had had to spit out the tough, disgusting peels.

I presided over washing the potatoes, splashing about in the icy water for a good hour. In the kitchen the food was cooked in three huge, sparkling clean, red copper boilers. I washed potatoes until one of these boilers was filled. By then, I was unable to move my frozen fingers. When I felt a burning pain, other women took over washing the potatoes for the next two cauldrons. In the meantime, four women carried the potatoes into the kitchen in large basins and poured them into the giant cauldrons. Once the cauldrons were full, they were sealed, and the thermometer attached to them indicated when the food was ready. If the head cook was in a good mood, she gave a dish full of bones to our *Anweiserin*, who distributed one or two pieces to each of us. All the meat had been removed and we could only chew on the bones, like dogs. Once, by chance, I found bone marrow in one of them.

We could rest for a few minutes before sweeping up the kitchen to make room for the next shipment of potatoes. At first the neighbouring farmers brought them and we just had to unload them from the cart, but later, larger shipments arrived and it was our job to store them in gigantic, hundred-metre-long pits. It took a lot of hard hacking at the ice before a few women could get in and toss out the potatoes. We collected them in sacks, placed them on a cart, and pushed it along the long, arduous path to the *Schälküche*.

It was December and my attire consisted of one slip, a silk dress and a spring coat; my stockings and trousers had long since gone to shreds from all the washing. Unlike the others, I had kept on washing. Most of the women were wearing unwashed underwear because they had neither the water nor the time for it, but I had both in the peeling place. When the potatoes were finally in the peeling kitchen, we could catch our breath and have our breakfast, bread that we'd saved from the evening before, toasted on the sides of the stove. With margarine spread on it, and potatoes, this was a tasty delicacy, though we had hardly swallowed before it was time to start peeling again.

These morning hours were the most pleasant times of the day. The *Schälküche* was the social club of the Lager. The *Blokova*, the doctor and the *Stubendienst* all came in to warm up and roast potatoes, and they brought the news and the newspapers they had stolen from the German staff. While someone was guarding the front door, we read the news we'd been starved for. We were mostly interested in the fighting in Budapest and what was going on in Hungary. I remember how comical it seemed when they read that in Budapest the enemy had been pushed back from the West Railway Station to the East Railway Station. We couldn't believe that this was true. We had no idea that our liberators were engaged in house-to-house fighting to gain ground.

We anxiously awaited the news even though the events seemed so distant that we could not see any connection between the fighting back home and our current fate. We worried about our loved ones who had stayed on in Budapest; were they still alive amid the terrible fighting, bombing and starvation? To the best of our knowledge, Zsófi's parents, my sister-in-law and Pali's dear old parents remained there – if indeed they had not died of grief over their son's deportation. I thought of them often.

While I was mechanically peeling, sitting beside the stove, my thoughts were always filled with the children who were out in the field, digging and hacking the icy ground. If it was particularly cold or windy, I was extremely distressed. Sometimes at noon, after dinner had been taken to the field, a few girls were carried back on the cart, most of the time unconscious, frozen or bleeding from some accident. I always looked at the cart with trepidation. Would they be my loved ones? Ági and Zsófi were still bearing up – albeit with difficulty and in misery – for now. The weaker ones were dropping, one after the other, and there were more and more sick people in the infirmary. It was awful to even enter it, yet I ran over there every day for a few minutes. "Auntie Anna! Auntie Anna!" I'd hear, the feeble voices of the sick girls calling me. From the secret pocket of my coat I would produce a stolen potato, carrot, kohlrabi, pushing them into their hands covertly. They were grateful, especially since that was the remedy they needed most, for many of their illnesses were caused by vitamin deficiency.

Girls, young women who had arrived from Auschwitz in good condition – since only the strong and healthy had been selected from there – were lying on lice-infested, rotting straw, starved to skeletons, helpless. They had stopped fighting the cold, hunger, lice and sickness. And what for? None of them suffered from a severe disease, let alone a fatal disease, yet they were perishing by the day, succumbing to diarrhea, abscesses, general weakness. The death toll kept increasing. As they complained about their ailments to me, I would console them, without much conviction, knowing there was no help for them. It almost broke my heart. That's when I saw my bitter prophecy realized: that here we would be digging each other's grave.

When someone died, Manci Indig from Várad and her team undressed the body completely, and when the dinner cart returned from the field, the corpse was thrown on top. Then they pulled the cart out of the Lager to a small forest, about two kilometres away. The young women dug a one-metre-deep hole at the foot of a tree and buried their workmates, friends, siblings.

There were already thirty graves in the small forest. Graves of the lovingly protected daughters of thirty mothers, the cherished darlings of thirty fathers. Young lives that had been extinguished so prematurely; how many dreams of a happy future had each of them held dear? One of the girls asked me in a weak voice, the day before her death, whether she should wear a long dress at her wedding when she went home to her fiancé. They were dreaming about bridal veils, a beautiful new home, and in their eternal home, they didn't even deserve a shroud or a coffin. Now their dreams were buried with them, and only the grim trees of this hated foreign land whispered farewell to them.

The girls who had to bury their companions there slowly got used to it. They no longer sobbed and shuddered at their sad duty. I understood more and more why the Slovak girls in Auschwitz had been so heartless. It was impossible to perform such acts in a way that allowed you to retain your humanity. Those who took these terrible experiences too much to heart perished, and those who wanted to live had to push and shove and do everything in their power, without scruples, to achieve this. The position in the peeling kitchen provided me and my loved ones with just such an opportunity to live.

The Death March

When I was still working outdoors, I was so dizzy with hunger that if Ági had not been there to catch me, I would have plunged into the deep ditch. At that point we had been starving for only a few weeks. Imagine then November and December! Everybody was emaciated, nothing but skin and bones. Our faces were grey from dirt, fatigue and starvation. Our sunken eyes had no expression left in them. Our hair and clothes were full of lice. Everyone had frostbitten feet and hands. Covered with rashes, abscesses, spots induced by vitamin deficiency, nobody even looked human anymore. I came to this conclusion one morning when, because of a great downpour, which luckily had not stopped by morning, the children stayed back. It had been so long since I'd had a chance to see them in daylight because they marched out in the pitch dark and returned in the pitch dark. This time, when I saw them during the day, I was speechless.

Ági and Zsófi had left Auschwitz in excellent shape, and back home they had been sweet, lovely creatures, radiant with youth and health. Now, at the age of twenty-two, they had become old women. The two dimples on Ági's cheeks had been replaced by two deep creases; her dreamy blue eyes were despondent. Zsófi was plagued by itch mites, with horrible, never-healing abscesses on her arm, and was in utmost misery. Herta, who used to be such a charming young woman – the cruel Grese had liked her well enough to make her a gift of a skirt – had become a skeleton with an unrecognizable grey face. Had we looked like this in Auschwitz, they would have sent all of us to the gas chamber, not bothering with selection. Fortunately, they didn't have a gas chamber here, though they did scare us with the prospect of it all the time. At the infirmary, we were told that whoever managed to stand on their feet should march out because there would be a selection; Mengele would arrive and take the weak ones back to Auschwitz to the crematorium. We didn't know, then, that they were no longer cremating anyone in Auschwitz. It was only much later that I found out that by the end of November the crematoria were in the process of being dismantled, to prevent the Soviets from finding evidence of the Germans' deplorable, diabolical cruelty. By then, it was all the same to us, whether we died here or there. What was the difference? There was no disputing, not even for a moment, that we would all perish.

Christmas was approaching. What we were expecting of it, I don't know, but it was rumoured that after Christmas we'd be taken somewhere else. Where? Why? We didn't know. Just away from here – that's all we desired. The girls were guessing what we would get for Christmas. We got bare Christmas trees that were set up in the two corners of our sad living quarters, most likely in mockery, but we did rest on this day, and we got goulash for dinner, in which we found the occasional piece of meat. It was a sad, miserable day for Ági. It was the anniversary of her engagement. She was very quiet all day, teary-eyed, her thoughts with her young husband. Was he still alive?

That evening, to our great joy, Dr. Eta invited the three of us for "coffee," and thus we spent Christmas evening sitting on chairs around a table. The other doctor, Iréne from Vienna, also invited an actress friend of hers from Vienna who sang for us, and we passed a pleasant evening there. We got coffee with sugar and our generous hostess served us potato salad with real onions and vinegar. We filled the dishes we had brought with us and ate and ate. Not only that, but we were also served, on the lid of a box, sandwiches spread with meat pâté. We couldn't believe our eyes. We ate about twenty each. Dr. Eta had given up her bread ration for three days to be able to provide this princely "stuff yourself to the gills" feast. I told her that if we made it home and she and her family were to be my guests for a year, I would still not be able to reciprocate for this evening. Once the evening ended, it felt that much worse to lie down on straw after having felt human for a while, sitting in a bright, warm room around a table, savouring the tastes of home.

Then, we were impatiently waiting for the New Year, for perhaps it would bring about a change in our fate. Had we had any inkling, we wouldn't have been looking forward to it so much. All the girls of my company came to wish me Happy New Year on New Year's morning. It almost broke my heart. Every one of them cried when I kissed them. "How lucky that there is at least one mum here who can kiss us, who can listen to our troubles," they sobbed. They knew very well that they were orphans, that they would never again see their parents.

Later, the *Lagerälteste* told us that we would probably soon be taken to factories. We were happy to receive this news, imagining working in heated rooms, being better fed. But the days kept passing and the drudgery continued, and we were still there.

One day in early January, when the company came back from the field and I ran to Ági with the soup I had saved from dinner, I found her crying. The thought struck me that there must be something really wrong if Ági was greeting me in tears. This child was goodness and tenderness personified. When, after the coldest and most miserable day, I had been anxiously awaiting her arrival, she would rush to me, smiling. "Weren't you cold, my Ágika?" I asked. "Oh, not at all, it was a very pleasant day." (All the while, she would be blue and shivering from the cold.) "Besides, all that's important," she said, "is that you, Mother, didn't have to march out. If I'm cold during the day, that's what I think of and I'm not so cold any more. And I wasn't hungry either, since I ate a little potato in the morning, and I had the leftover bread from last night as my snack."

That was her daily refrain. In the evenings, when we both had a supper break, our *Anweiserin* let her stay with me and warm up in the *Schälküche*. She brought along her supper, and basically that was all the time we spent together the whole day. That's when she would relate what had happened outdoors, who had done her job well, who hadn't (she was an excellent worker), what they were cooking (in theory), and who was sick and had to be brought back by cart. I also told her about what I had heard in the social club, and we passed an agreeable little hour together. I always sent her to bed shortly after, since the poor dear was so wrecked and exhausted. When I went to bed as well, sometimes not until midnight, she was sleeping soundly. I snuggled up to her and she would embrace me happily even in her dreams.

And now, my good little daughter was crying. At my anxious questioning, she admitted that her legs had been awfully sore for days and she could hardly get up in the morning. Zsófi and Herta had had to practically carry her and drag her to the work site. Once there, her legs somehow could move again, but they would start aching again on the way home. When she lay down to rest, the pains associated with the frostbite compounded the muscular aches. "Why didn't you show them to Eta?" I asked in despair. "I did," she replied, "she's been giving me painkillers every morning to help me get on my feet." "Why didn't you stay in the infirmary?" I sobbed along with her. "Because there are so many lice there that I wouldn't lie down in that place for the world! Everybody deteriorates there; they pick up new diseases and they never leave that place again, except to go to the little forest."

I ran to Eta and reproached her for not having mentioned Ági's condition. In her defense, she said Ági wouldn't let her and that she had given her word of honour not to trouble me with it. "It was going to pass," she said. "She has muscular inflammation in both legs, caused by lifting the heavy wooden clogs." She just needed to lie down, she said, and I should convince her to do that.

The next morning, Ági could not get to her feet at all, and no matter how much she feared it, and rightly so, we made her lie down in the infirmary. Eta announced that if Ági recovered, she would become her *Stubendienst* and would not have to go out to the field again. This, of course, would have been a great stroke of luck, would have meant a warm room and better food. However, in spite of how good it must have felt to lie down and rest, Ági's legs were not improving, and the lice were driving her crazy. Two of her close friends were lying next to her; one, Ily, was Pali's niece. She had been staying in the infirmary for months because of abscesses. She was just skin and bones, and even though Eta treated her and bandaged her very conscientiously, the abscesses didn't heal and she got weaker by the day. I was bringing her "vitamins" in vain; she couldn't eat any more. I still get the shivers when I think of her sad end.

~

We still held the view that the Soviets were approaching and that we'd be taken away from there. We believed it and yet we didn't. It was unimaginable to us that we would really be liberated from our captivity. In the meantime, we worried that if our liberators approached, our guards would slaughter us before they fled themselves.

Both fearfully and hopefully, we whispered about the events to come. The Lager showed no signs of change. Instead, the Germans started building. That is to say, around the middle of January, a new building was brought into the Lager. No matter how strange it sounds, that's what happened. It was a whole building, dismantled into pieces that took hours to assemble, complete with doors, windows and electrical lighting. The German women and soldiers lived in small ready made houses of this kind. They seemed like little fairytale cottages. Anytime we looked at their windows, covered in flowery curtains, our hearts ached with the reminder of home.

This time, however, they were bringing in parts of a larger building, which turned out to be a new hospital. It was ready in a day, and moreover, it had proper bunks outfitted with pallets and pillows. This seemed like a heavenly vision to the sick women lying on lice-infested straw. The patients were transferred over, bathed, disinfected, deloused and wrapped in brand new blankets. The transfer, however, meant that sick women had to run, at least those who were able to, across the yard, naked and wrapped in only a blanket, on January 17 in the extreme cold. Ági plodded along miserably, leaning on me, and by the next day she was running a fever of 39 degrees Celsius.

All their belongings were kept behind to prevent lice from getting into the pristine quarters, and they were promised they would get them all back, disinfected. The days passed and this didn't happen. They were lying on the bunks, wrapped only in a blanket. We weren't allowed to visit the patients. Each time I looked through the window to see Ági and hand her some food, the sight almost broke my heart. Sometimes, with great difficulty, she got up off the bed and dragged herself to the window to be able to talk to me. She would tell me what a nice place the hospital was, the food better and plentiful; they were being washed and, most importantly, there were no lice. Her appetite was excellent and she was able to satisfy it as well, with both Dr. Eta and me always feeding her. We were full of hope that she would recover soon.

The new hospital had been in place for five days when we were thunderstruck by the news that we would be taken away. My first thought was that Ági and the rest of the patients didn't have any clothes. I ran to the disinfecting station, luckily headed by my friend from Miskolc, Lili Glück, and gathered whatever I could for her and Ily: underwear, dresses, coats, sweaters. The only thing I couldn't get hold of was shoes, and Ági was barefoot.

That day, as usual, the company was out working in the field. When they came back and went into the barn, the *Lagerälteste* announced that we would be taking off in an hour. We didn't need to pack – since we had nothing – yet it hit us like a bombshell that we would have to get ready so fast and leave late in the evening.

My only concern was what was going to happen to the sick. Dr.

Eta went to find out from the *Lagerälteste*. So far, the command was that the sick would stay, she reported, but she predicted a dark future for them, so Ági had better get up and come with us. Never before or since have I been as desperate as I was at that time. Forcing myself to be calm, I went to see Ági and asked her to get up and try to walk. She got out of bed, but she could hardly make it over to the window.

"I would like you to come, my Ágika. It would be better for you to go with our friends than to stay behind with the sick," I said.

"I can't, no matter how hard I try," she answered despondently.

"Then we are both going to stay," I replied, smiling at her. "You know that, being a potato peeler, I am also considered to be sick, so I have the right to stay."

I was, of course, condemning myself to death along with her, but the main thing was that Ági not suspect anything. There was not a shadow of a doubt in my mind that the ones who stayed behind would be executed.

Next, I started figuring out where we should hide once the company departed. Maybe in the potato pit. We wouldn't starve to death there, and once everyone was gone, we could come out. Oh, if only I had carried out my plan and hidden in the potato pit or somewhere in the straw! We would have been spared so much, and today I would be together with Ági. But before I had a chance, a cart sped into the yard, carrying the gravely ill from the town of Schlesiersee. They had needed operations and been taken to the local hospital, which was considered very lucky, for they were treated very decently there and many of them returned fully recovered and dressed in proper clothes. These patients told us that they had been brought back because the Soviets were approaching and the town had been evacuated. Our joy was great, but so was our panic. As I mentioned, we had every reason to fear that if our rescuers were indeed approaching, our hangmen would annihilate us all.

The soldiers guarding the patients arrived with a new command: everybody, including the sick, had to be on their way; no one was allowed to stay at the farm. Those who couldn't walk were to be pushed by the healthy ones on the little wheelbarrows that were used for carrying sand.

I thought I would go out of my mind. I knew that all the women were so weak that they could hardly walk themselves, let alone push the sick on wheelbarrows in front of them. I ran around frantically looking for a pair of shoes. At last, Eta managed to get a pair of narrow French shoes with pointed toes, and I struggled to put them on Ági's pained feet. I then raised my voice and spoke firmly to her, while my heart was breaking, "My Ágika, you've got to come; your life is at stake." She did. God performed a miracle – not for the first time, and not for the last time.

Eta gave her three painkillers and Zsófi and I supported her on either side. We were ready to leave. We were told that we would have to walk a hundred kilometres before our first place of rest. It didn't matter who was sick and who wasn't, who was able to set out and who wasn't, because one thing was for certain – none of us would survive that in such a starved state in the cold of January. They were in such a hurry that they didn't even serve us supper, although meat and potatoes were cooking in the cauldrons. They distributed only bread, nothing else. Each row of five received two loaves; we were sent on our way with only forty decagrams of bread each, on a march of one hundred kilometres.

I should have joined the house company, to which I belonged. Had we left with them, maybe our lives would have taken a different turn, but all our friends were in the fourth company and they vowed to carry Ági on their backs if necessary. We stayed with them. The *Blokova* gave the members of the house company as many loaves of bread as they could carry, four or five per person. They also got margarine and even meat. We, on the other hand, started off with rumbling stomachs. I didn't even have time to fill the hidden pockets of my coat with raw potatoes, although I wouldn't have been able to carry them anyway; even the small piece of bread was hard enough to carry.

I will never forget that march. I think I will be haunted by the horrible sight even on my death bed. It would have made the perfect illustration for Dante's *Inferno*. At the front, the stronger young women were pushing the sick in wheelbarrows. In the awful cold January night, naked and wrapped only in blankets, the sick screamed that they were freezing. In the tiny wheelbarrows, they could not even sit. They squatted. Soon they were in such a state that they didn't scream any more, nor did they say a word; they sank into a fatal lethargy.

The companies marched behind them. Everyone looked like they had a sort of hood on, with the same grey blanket around their shoulders. We looked more like ghosts than human beings.

We marched about six kilometres back to the station we had arrived at when we came from Auschwitz: Schlesiersee. Ági had withstood the trip quite well so far. The whole town was full of people fleeing and soldiers retreating. This would have been an excellent opportunity to escape because we spent the whole night standing at the station, and they couldn't have cared less about us. It was pitch dark and the houses were empty. If we had bolted into one of these houses, we would have been liberated in a couple of hours. Perhaps we were cowards. Up to that point, nobody had fled from our ranks.

We were sleeping standing up, leaning against each other, until we sensed that our carefully guarded treasure, our bread, was slipping out of our hands. Sometimes it had already landed in the snow. The feeling of the bread falling jolted us awake endlessly, and it was a hellish night.

Then, all of a sudden, our escorts declared that we had taken the wrong road and they made us turn back. The third and most torturous act of our tragedy – the march – began. The ghetto was the prologue of our drama, Auschwitz was the first act, after which, we thought, our fate couldn't get any worse. But the second act, Schlesiersee – with its hated windmills, digging our own graves and dreadful starvation that almost killed us all – was much more horrid. Now that we were expecting that being taken somewhere else would mean a change for the better, we came to the realization that the third act was going to be the fitting end to the tragedy. According to the formula of the ancient Greek tragedies, all of the characters are dead by the time the curtain falls. We must perish – there was no escaping it.

In the morning when it grew light, the utterly exhausted women who were pushing the wheelbarrows came to the realization that fourteen of the sick, whom they had believed to be sleeping, were actually dreaming their eternal dreams. They had frozen to death.

We stopped at the edge of a forest. The soldiers accompanying us dug a ditch that was hardly half a metre deep and the women threw in the corpses of their young comrades who, only a few hours before, had been alive and hopeful. Not all of them were dead yet; I saw it with my own eyes. One of the "corpses" lifted an arm when she was being thrown into the ditch. I started shouting, but a soldier gestured me to stop. She is going to die anyway; it makes no difference to her. She was no longer considered a human being from whom a little extra work could still be squeezed out, and she was buried alive. We were all affected by this, crying, wailing, seeing our own fate in each tragedy.

We continued on, haunted. All of a sudden, from the Polish company that was marching ahead of us, we saw a woman run out of the formation to the field and lie down. Two women rushed to her, bent over her and fussed with something for a few minutes. Then, we heard the faint sound of a baby crying. It curdled our blood. The woman rose to her feet, dragged herself back to the line and, leaving her baby behind, marched on.

We had scarcely moved when the leader declared that those who couldn't walk should get on the cart behind us. The weak and the sick eagerly grabbed at the chance, and thirty-eight women got on the cart. Dr. Iréne was among them. I wondered for a moment whether I should have Ági sit there, since she could barely walk, yet I decided that I wouldn't let her leave my side. At the foot of a hill, the cart stayed behind, and then thirty-eight gunshots sounded. We practically froze. We stared at each other, unable to utter a word. We had had many good friends sitting on that cart, among them Ily, the niece of Ági's husband, and my dear girlfriend from the *Schälküche*, a few friends from Szatmár, and the girls from the infirmary to whom I had brought "vitamins" so many times.

Dr. Eta, frightened, rushed over to us to find out if Ági had been on the cart. She was relieved to see that Ági was with me but was extremely worried about the fate of her colleague, Dr. Iréne. Could she really have been shot, too? At last Dr. Iréne arrived, together with the murderous soldiers, pale as death, staggering. She later related to Eta that the soldiers had dug a deep ditch, lined the sick women up beside it, and shot them so that they fell into it. This was a well-tested German recipe that had been used many times in the Ukraine on our men but we could never have believed it possible that we women would be treated the same way, not even by these sadistic German murderers, who had shed all traces of humanity. Even the soldiers who had behaved relatively decently during work detail had now gone wild, from the commanding officer on down. They beat and battered everyone who stepped out of the line.

We had witnessed what awaited those who weren't able to march on and lagged behind. Only God can tell how much I suffered because of Ági who, with a smile, staggered along beside me. Her scared eyes were constantly watching me to see whether I, too, was still able to carry on.

On this first day, we ate only a few bites from our meagre bread supply. We stopped in a village, where each of us was handed about three cooked potatoes. A few warm bites for our withered innards. Then we marched on, and it was late at night by the time we arrived in front of a barn in a big village. After standing around for a few hours, asleep on our feet, we were at last allowed into our night lodgings. The space could accommodate only about four hundred, so the thousand of us could get in only by clambering over top of one another. Not caring in the least that some people broke an arm or a leg in the scuffle, people pushed each other into the barn. Those who fell were trampled on. No one cared about anyone else. We had to fight to get inside and not lose one another in the dark, in the scuffle, in the mayhem. Ági and I got in at last, carried forward by the surge, and we hid in a corner to avoid being trampled to death by the others. Holding each other by the hand, we lay down and, thanks to our terrible exhaustion, fell asleep.

When the morning arrived, we awoke to a new day and new traumas. We suffered, putting the tight shoes on Ági's swollen, aching feet, until, thanks to Eta's additional painkillers, she could get going. We experienced awful hunger, and it took immense will power to save a small piece of bread for the next day. We trembled as we watched our bread supply diminish; we knew that once it was finished, we'd be finished too. Women were dropping one after the other, wavering and then falling down. Their sister or friend would try to pull them to their feet and drag them along, but they just couldn't. They didn't have any strength left to walk either. If a woman stayed by the roadside, we were informed, by the sound of a gunshot, that there were fewer of us again. We were all terrified.

Suddenly – fortunately not while we were marching but during a rest period – I felt that I was getting weak. The world went black before my eyes, I crumpled to the ground, and when I woke up, a crying Ági, Herta and Magda were desperately rubbing my face and chest with snow. I felt Ági's tears on me and I got to my feet saying, "Nothing is the matter!" From that time on, I could always sense Ági's alarmed glances, wondering if I would collapse again. Had I fainted during the march, I would have been shot to death.

There was one thought nagging constantly at my brain – that I would collapse and Ági would stay behind for my sake. I asked her a hundred times, "My Ágika, do you promise to march on if I collapse?" but she only raised her tearful blue eyes to me, and I knew she would not leave me behind by the side of the road. I was desperately afraid that she would stay behind because of me and the German beasts would shoot us both. I couldn't get rid of this thought; it gave me strength and I went on for the third day. Always the same deathly exhaustion; in the evening, dropping down in a barn into a deep, dreamless sleep; in the morning, waking up to the horrible reality, and always the firm conviction that this would be my last day. That day, two sweet sisters from Szatmár, Ági and Kató Kohn, seventeen and eighteen years old, collapsed. Two charming, dear children. At that point, we hadn't eaten for at least two days. On the verge of fainting from hunger, we marched and marched, condemned to death.

There were a few braver souls, mostly among the women from Máramaros, who dared to enter a German house here and there, begging for food or stealing it. Even if they were beaten when found out, they didn't care. It was worth it. They managed to get a bite of bread, maybe prolonging their life by an hour or so.

The road was full of German refugees. These country folk had loaded their bare necessities onto carts and were eating bacon and drinking, surrounded by pillows and comforters. They looked at us in amazement. If one of them took pity on us starving, grey-faced women by tossing a piece of bread or a bacon rind, a hundred people grabbed at once, and usually it would land on the ground and be trodden on or a soldier would snatch it from the hand of the person who somehow managed to catch it, rudely berate the German peasant who had thrown it, and beat us.

Why? Surely they were well aware of what we did not know then, that the Soviets were on their heels. They should have repented of their base crimes and set those who were still alive free, to go wherever they wished. What harm could we have done them even if we were free? I think they felt their demise was near and wanted to torture us as long as they could. The sound of their truncheons thudded on our backs.

We were thinking more and more of escaping. But how? What would happen to someone who stayed behind in a German village, looking so ghastly, without papers and money? I couldn't imagine that fugitives like us would not be recognized and arrested right away, which would naturally be followed by being shot. In addition, we suffered from herd mentality, unwilling to leave the group. After all, we were afraid of our own shadows; how could we tackle the thousand dangers of an escape? Even though this would have been the only way out, we didn't dare to risk it.

The soldiers became more alert, watching us constantly, and if someone so much as made a step out of formation, they were instantly beside them, beating them. We were allowed to attend to our bodily needs only during the rest periods, but as we hadn't been eating for days there was less and less call for this. Natural biological functions started to come to a halt in our starved, desiccated bodies. We became like machines that will operate for a while without being oiled, even though they squeak when they start moving. We lifted our feet mechanically, driven by the instinct to live; we kept going unconsciously just because we had been set into motion and the machine hadn't wound down yet.

On the fourth day, the soldiers told us that we would have to cross the Oder River. We passed through two larger towns before we reached the Oder. The first one was Unruhstadt and the second was Züllichau. It was the same scene everywhere: people racing against the retreating army. In many places, we were pushed off the main roads onto dirt roads, lest we impede the progress of the refugees. Thousands of refugees moved on carts, on foot, pulling their bundles behind them on sleds. What a joy it was to see our swastika-wearing murderers, intoxicated with victory, forced to share this fate. They had to leave their homes behind, tying whatever they could salvage into bundles, carrying their many children with them, wandering along the highways for days like beggars who had been turned away, just like us.

But they had warm clothing. They had food.

As the days went on, Zsófi found the march harder and harder to endure and she decided to escape. She asked us to go with her, and we made up our minds to do so. When we reached the end of Unruhstadt, Zsófi nudged me, and I watched as she slipped into the last house in town. By the time I looked around to alert Ági, the guard was right beside us and we could not jump out of the line. Zsófi stayed behind. We envied her and worried about her at the same time.

We had scarcely walked for a couple of hours when who should be joining us but Zsófi. I was so surprised I could hardly speak. She relayed that when she noticed she was by herself, she stepped out of the house. A car full of German soldiers was sitting there. She walked over and asked them to take her with them because she couldn't walk and had lost her group. Zsófi was pretty, blond and spoke good German, so the soldiers let her climb into the car. They gave her food and drink, and they would have kept her with them, but to Zsófi's misfortune they followed the same route we did and when they spotted our company, the soldiers were afraid that they would get into trouble, so they let Zsófi out. Nevertheless, this adventure gave her the courage to try another escape, and we did not discard our plan.

The next day, we reached Züllichau, on the banks of the Oder. Here, suddenly, Zsófi and three other girls from her row were gone. They most likely had signalled to us, but we must not have noticed in the dark. Even though I was very worried about Zsófi, I gave her credit for having the good sense to escape on this side of the Oder and most likely be liberated sooner, as long as they were not caught and shot.

Escaping was not as easy as this might make it seem. Many had tried to enter German houses but were thrown out; there was the odd German family that provided something to eat, but there was none that would let us stay. That meant you could only slip into a house that was surrounded by farm buildings, where you could hide and not be noticed. I had come to this conclusion long before, and I was thinking more and more about making an escape. After all, what choice did we have? If we continued on, we'd eventually collapse and be shot. If we got caught, we would also get shot, but there was, nonetheless, a faint ray of hope of getting away. I'm not sure if I believed that we would actually escape and return home.

Meanwhile, we were driven so hard that we were not even allowed to stop for a minute. That's when I became familiar with the torments of Tantalus. We were parched with thirst, yet we were wading through snow up to our knees and did not have enough time to bend down for a handful. Bending down meant breaking stride. Someone stepping over you meant being left behind. That, of course, meant the end.

We kept marching and marching, hungry and thirsty, stumbling in the snow through villages and forests; our mouths were dry from thirst, our eyes hollow from hunger, and we kept dragging ourselves further and further. Where to? Why? Nobody knew.

It went on like this for six days. On that sixth day, our dear and beloved friend from Nagyvárad, Bözsi Kovács, fell out of our row of five. Herta had been carrying her because Ági and I could hardly move ourselves, but Herta got so exhausted that she had to leave her friend by the roadside. She was shot by a soldier right before Herta's eyes. This had a terrible impact on us. Bözsi had been the strongest, most optimistic one of our group. She was convinced that she would get back home to the husband she adored – who was in Auschwitz – and she was preparing for a new start to a happy life. We grieved bitterly and yet continued on, but how long could we last?

We hadn't eaten a bite in three days when we found a sack of wheat in a barn, from which – at the risk of being killed – we filled our pockets. Blessed wheat. God's greatest gift. We ate a handful, filling our empty stomachs fairly well. Dr. Eta shared her last bit of food with us as well. We watched enviously as some of the girls ate a raw potato or turnip. Although those who belonged to the house company still had some food, they wouldn't give a bite to anyone because their lives depended on how long they could endure. I tried to use my last bite of bread to save my friend from Várad. I pushed it into her mouth and she rallied a bit and walked with us for another hour. She collapsed later. We knew that none of us would last long, yet everybody was trying to prolong their lives.

At last, after having crossed the Oder on the evening of the sixth day, January 28, they made us stop outside of a bigger town and told us that we had reached our destination. Our first major place of rest! We were full of hope that we would be allowed to stay there and maybe, at last, we'd be given something to eat. However, after a long wait, we were on our way again and we marched into the town of Grünberg. We were taken into a Lager that had originally been built for the forced labourers of a textile factory. We found ourselves in a huge, well-heated room with a long wash basin down the middle and many bunk beds on each side. Beside each bed for two was a small wardrobe. We thought we had woken from a bad dream to find ourselves in paradise. Warmth! A chance to wash ourselves! And most likely food as well! In this last wish we were disappointed. They didn't give us anything to eat. I managed to put Ági to bed beside Dr. Eta, but there was no room left for me. I lay down on the stone floor, but what did I care. The important thing was that Ági had a bed; I slept just fine where I was.

Next morning, it was out to the yard to form up our rows of five. I dreaded the thought of being sent on my way again. For once, I was pleasantly surprised. They distributed soup, an excellent potato soup to boot, a good half a litre of it. When we finished, we were sent back to the Lager with word that we were allowed to have a day's rest there. What bliss it was to lie down for a day! To stretch our aching, frozen limbs in a warm room. This was the first time we had been in a heated room since leaving home eight months earlier. It became that much harder to think that tomorrow we would continue on.

That evening, Ica Klein from Tiszapolgár, a friend I had made in Auschwitz, invited me to sleep on her "organized" straw pallet. Yet, in the morning, I felt so weak that I told her my time on this earth would end on this day. It was Monday again, and it had been a week since we had left the farm, during which time all we had eaten was forty decagrams of bread, a handful of wheat, and half a litre of soup. I was feeling so weak that I could hardly get on my feet, and Ica was in the same state. Ági had had a better rest. Eta gave her a small piece of bread with margarine for breakfast, and a girl from Szatmár, Klári Treiszer, gave her a pair of woollen socks to prevent her aching feet from getting cold.

We started on our way. I was ready to face death. I told Herta that all three of us should try to flee, as I could not bear it any longer, but she said that as long as she could walk she would; she was not going to tamper with her fate. Ági was also afraid of escaping, but I was continuously mulling it over because I knew I was about to collapse. I feared, as I had earlier, that Ági would stay behind with me.

We marched through the streets of Grünberg again, this time in daylight. There was not much sign of the panic that had previously accompanied us on our path. The stores, pastry shops and coffee houses were open. Behind their windows, happy people were sitting and eating. My God! They were having coffee! And they were eating snow-white buns with it! All along the street, people stared at us. We were such an awful sight that perhaps we even drew a few sympathetic glances. I wouldn't have believed, then, that I would ever again sit in the window of such a pastry shop, properly dressed, with money in my pocket the way these people were. It was too beautiful even for a dream.

I was incapable of walking. "My Ágika, let us flee!" I implored. But she didn't dare. Sensing that I was about to collapse, and dreading to be shot in front of Ági and having her fall behind because of me and suffer the same fate, I made my decision. In the second village past Grünberg, I noticed that our guard was not nearby. I signalled Ági and with a quick resolve I sprang through the doorway of a German house. I was hoping that Ági was following me. Prepared for the worst, not knowing whether the guard had noticed me, I just kept going.

In that moment, something extremely strange happened to me.

My being somehow split in two. Every movement of my body was controlled only by a survival instinct, while my mind was separate, watching what would transpire. I felt, let's say, as if I was sitting in a movie theatre watching a strange heroine, her adventures, and how her fate unfolded. Ági did not follow me. I was so desperate, and so certain that on this day, January 29, my life would come to an end. I was no longer interested in my own escape. What for? Without Ági? Alone? I was interested, instead, in the problem of whether a despised, persecuted, dreadful-looking Jewish woman could escape from the clutches of German soldiers in the middle of Germany.

Alone

I see myself with a hunched back, emaciated and grey, as I am shuf-
fling my aching, broken feet in the strange yard of a strange German
house. I look around and I don't see anyone. I quickly slip into an outhouse and I stand there, still waiting for Ági to rush after me, while
our company marches by. The street grows silent. I am calm, my heart
not even pounding any harder than usual. It just aches, aches for Ági.
Maybe this way she will be saved, I think. After all, she is young and
tough, and she will weather the trip better if she doesn't have to worry
about me all the time. Today I would have collapsed for sure, and
what if I had been shot in front of her?

I don't know how long I was standing in the outhouse. After some
time, I emerged, unfortunately too soon because after a few steps in
the yard I came face to face with three German women. They looked
at me, open-mouthed. "I'm hungry," I said. "I haven't eaten for three
days, I'd like to have some bread." In response, the three women scattered. Two entered the house – maybe to get bread? The third one, on
the other hand, frantically rushed out to the street, and I immediately
sensed that she would fetch a soldier. By myself in the yard for a few
moments, I looked around and quickly decided to spring into a sort
of barn and hide in the straw. I didn't have much time, so I lay down
right beside the door, covering myself with a lot of straw and with a
laundry basket that was sitting there. I even took care not to turn the

basket upside down, which might have looked suspicious, and I put it on top of me right side up.

As soon as I was done, a lot of people rushed into the barn, making a great clamour. Of course I couldn't see, but I heard everything. Unbelievable as it may sound, in this moment, knowing that I would be killed within minutes, I was waiting with perfect calm for the events to unfold. A German soldier was swearing as he scattered the straw; to my fright, I recognized his voice as belonging to one of our meanest guards. He even lifted the laundry basket but still he didn't find me. I held my breath, lying there in such stillness that not a single straw rustled.

The whole group rushed out to the yard, angry and swearing, to keep searching for me. Then, just when I thought I was safe, I heard the triumphant shout of a child right beside me. "Da ist sie! Da ist sie!" (Here she is!) Once more, the crowd charged in. After all, a manhunt was free entertainment for the good village folks.

The German soldier dragged me out from under the straw and started beating me. Sporting a Hitler moustache, his face burning with hatred, he was leaning over me, beating me with increasing fervour, screaming at me to get up and go with him. "I'm not going, I'm not able to walk! I beg you, just shoot me!" But with bloodshot eyes, foaming at the mouth, he just went on beating and hitting me anyplace he could – my head, my face, my hands that were flailing as I tried to protect myself.

To this day, I don't understand why he wouldn't shoot me. Perhaps he didn't want to shoot a defenceless woman in front of so many witnesses. I don't know. He just kept on beating me so brutally that my head was covered in blood. I remained conscious and all I could think of was how lucky it was that Ági hadn't followed me, that she wasn't being beaten to death by this devil. While I was saying goodbye to my loved ones in my mind, the soldier pulled me out of the barn to the yard, held me by the head, and delivered one huge blow to my left eye, watching to see whether I was still alive. I was holding my breath and pretending to be dead. "Kaputt!" he shouted. He tore the number – 71919 – off my jacket and ordered the woman who had fetched him to wait for a couple of hours for me to freeze before they buried me. "Is there someone who can inter her?" he asked. "Yes," the woman answered, "my husband will be back by evening and he'll tend to it." The soldier covered me with my grey blanket and, satisfied with a job well done, hurried after his company, which by now was a good distance ahead.

The women were standing at my side for a few minutes, then got tired of the spectacle and went back to what they'd been doing before. I was just lying there, petrified, beaten half to death and blind in one eye, or at least that's what I believed at the time. I could only open one eye. I felt a hellish, searing pain in the other, and a thick layer of blood covered my whole face. I lay there motionless. It almost felt good to rest on the icy snow, cooling my trembling body.

I must have been lying there without moving for one or two hours when I tried to move my arm to wipe the blood off my face. I couldn't lift my arm. My body was losing heat, and it flashed through my mind that if I wasn't careful, I could fall asleep, freeze from the cold, and be buried alive. All of a sudden, with a mighty effort, I sat up. The women must have been looking through the kitchen window as their corpse resurrected. They rushed over to me, scared, discussing what they should do. They had been given orders to bury a dead woman, but what to do with a live fugitive? Their German mentality, accustomed to obeying orders, was not able to decide. I told them off for calling the soldier when all I'd asked for was a little bit of bread. They were a bit regretful, I thought, and they decided not to report me to the authorities as long as I disappeared right away, and they could claim that I had escaped.

I would have left without much encouragement, but I couldn't. I told them what I'd had to eat for the last week and asked for a hot coffee or a bite of bread so I could move on. They didn't give me anything. I begged, in vain, for even a sip of water. They didn't want to, or they didn't dare to, I don't know. Even two hours later, I was still sitting in the snow without having been given a bite to eat, and I was trying to cool my burning thirst and my feverish, blistered lips with a handful of snow.

Meanwhile a few neighbours showed up, having heard about the interesting occurrence. They surrounded me and kept on asking how I had happened to get there. I told them that I had not been able to march anymore and I had stayed behind. "I have to get back to Grünberg, to the Lager," I said. "If you give me something to eat, I'll be on my way."

Then, the same kid who had found me in the barn, raised on a diet of Hitlerian hatred and hungry for a manhunt, brought two German soldiers from the street. One stated that if I didn't leave the village in five minutes, he would shoot me. He took out his watch while the other one suggested that maybe they should hang me at night, which would be lots of fun. I started to feel rather uncomfortable. Although I had long ago resigned myself to being shot, and would maybe even have been glad to have it over with, death by hanging was another matter. With great difficulty I got up and, slowly, started to head back.

I kept cautiously glancing back to see whether I was being followed or about to be shot in the back, but no one followed me. I was on the highway again, beaten up, one-eyed, hungry, cold, but free. The only thing freedom meant for the time being was that I could sit down in the snow beside a ditch whenever I wanted. No one was forcing me to keep moving and I could eat a handful of snow at my leisure if I felt like it. At any moment, however, I had to be prepared to be detained because of my suspicious looks. It soon grew dark, there were very few people on the road, and they didn't care much about a limping and shrivelled little old woman.

I remembered that I first had to go through a forest before a village, the first one past Grünberg. I wanted to reach it so as to avoid spending the night on the highway. I didn't give any thought to what I was going to do once I got there. After what had happened, I didn't dare enter a German house. I entrusted myself to fate and slowly, in a couple of hours, I arrived in the village. Streets branched off to either side of the road. Which way should I turn? Looking around, I saw that there was a military vehicle sitting to the right. That way looked hopeless but there seemed to be more safety to the left, with only two soldiers loitering around in that direction. Therefore, I took that turn. I had always believed in God, but on this day and during my adventures to come, I was under the impression that God was leading me by the hand. Whenever there was a fork in the road, I made the right choice and whenever I had to speak, I said the right thing.

I started off, passed a few houses, and then came across a stable-like building. Nobody saw me quickly slip inside. I went through a tiny door and found myself in a two-by-three-metre, empty, window-less room, with straw spread on the floor. I didn't think twice. I collapsed on the straw, covered myself with the blessed grey blanket, and fell into a deep sleep within seconds, which was no wonder, after the excitements I had lived through.

I don't know how long I had been sleeping when I awoke to a conversation and air filtering in. I could distinguish the voices of a woman and a child, and that of a man who said that he would wake them on time in the morning so that they could continue on their way. From these words, I understood that German refugees had been put up in the room next to me. I could make out that I was in a tiny stall that was part of the stable, separated only by a huge box filled with oats. It was used as the quarters for smaller animals, perhaps sheep, but it was empty, and I could have a good night's sleep there.

It was daylight when I woke to hear my neighbours being roused from sleep. The male voice from the previous evening encouraged them to get up, get packed and go to the house for breakfast. I also got myself ready, which consisted of putting my boots on my broken feet and shaking off the straw. I did this quietly, so as to not make the tiniest noise. I did not want them to notice that there was someone in the stall.

At last, after minutes that seemed like years, I heard my neighbours leave the stable. I got up and very carefully snuck to the door and looked outside. I didn't see anyone, but in front of the door there was a small sled with three suitcases on it – two large ones and a small one. Without hesitation, I stepped outside and grabbed the small, blue fibre suitcase, hid it under my clothing and calmly strode out of the yard.

Two girls were chatting at the corner, but they didn't even look my way. I walked on with the suitcase, which was alas terribly heavy. I suspected that it contained food, bread and bacon. I still hadn't eaten in days. The very thought of food filled me with a terrible weakness and I couldn't keep on going. I was standing at the same crossroads as the night before, except this time I couldn't ponder too long which way to go. I could hardly stand, the suitcase pulling me down, and now I was scared of being chased for the stolen suitcase. Without a moment's thought, I went inside the first property on the left side of the road.

It looked like a larger farm with a lot of outbuildings, but I wasn't able to make it as far as the barn. Although I risked being seen, I sat down in the yard, beside the oven. For a few minutes I didn't have enough strength to open the little suitcase to look at its contents, but then I tried to open the lock with my beaten blue, swollen, sore-covered hands. At last it opened, but to my bitter disappointment it was jam-packed with clothes. I almost started to cry at the sight. I kept searching and among the children's clothes and ladies' underwear I came across two honey buns. I thought it was a mirage but no, this was reality, and I bit into my first bite of food in four days. I didn't eat voraciously. I ate morsel by morsel to make it last and to spare my shrivelled stomach. Engrossed in this activity, I didn't even notice that someone was standing in front of me. I soon sensed that I was being watched, looked up in fright and saw a woman standing there. She didn't say a word, just turned around and ran off.

Here comes trouble, I thought. Only then did it cross my mind that if the woman reported me and handed me over to the authorities, I would be hanged without a doubt, if not for escaping, then for stealing a suitcase from a refugee. After all, we were under martial law. I concluded that it didn't matter, and it was worth it to be able to eat a few bites of something sweet, which every cell in my body had been craving, before my probable demise. I had hardly finished this thought when the same woman was standing in front of me again. She was holding a large mug of steaming hot coffee in one hand and a half-metre slice of bread in the other. There were tears running down her face straight into the coffee.

My God, what this felt like!

An encounter with human compassion. This felt even better than the food I had so fervently desired. The woman pushed the mug into my hand and I started to drink, feeling I was in heaven. That sugarless, hot liquid raced through my body, warmed my empty stomach, and most likely turned into blood inside me.

When I finished slowly drinking it all, she took the mug away and rushed into the house and filled it up again. Oh, may the good God bless her every step and lead her back to her home! She too was a prisoner, a Polish Christian working on a German farm. She asked me quickly, in a whisper, where I was going, who I was and what I was planning to do. I asked her to keep me there, to hide me somewhere, and she agreed right away. Luckily it was still early in the morning, there was no one on the highway, and she could easily take me over to one of the barns. With suitcase in hand, I climbed on top of a thresher in just seconds, from where I worked my way up to the hayloft. If today, when I am strong and healthy, someone asked me to repeat this feat, there is no way I could do it again, but God was by my side and helped me with his strength where my own strength was at a low ebb.

The woman brought me a comforter and a pillow. A real eider pillow, the likes of which I hadn't seen in eight months, and she made up a fine bed for me in the hay. I sifted through the contents of the suitcase at my leisure and came across some cheap, gaudy beads and jewellery in an envelope. I looked them over, thinking that they would be welcomed by the Polish woman's children – she told me that she had four little kids – and along with the children's clothing I set aside for her everything I didn't need. Suddenly, a thick, gold chain and a smaller gold chain fell from the envelope into my lap. I quickly stuck these in my hidden pocket, thinking that if I ran into trouble they might come in handy.

After this, I changed my clothes from head to toe. I only then realized how skinny I was, because the clothes in the suitcase were made to fit such a tiny, slim figure that back home they wouldn't have fit on my arm, never mind around my waist. Not only did they fit, they were too loose. At last I had clean, decent underwear and good clothes on, and two extra sets of everything still in the suitcase. With a pair of fine woollen stockings on my feet, the boots did not chafe my sore heels the way they had before. I was full, I had extra provisions of bread, and on top of this I had gold, a thick gold chain. Croesus couldn't have felt as rich as I did right then.

Then, for the first time, I started crying bitterly because I didn't have Ági with me. Up to that moment, I had been grateful to God that we hadn't fled together. I thought about it a thousand times, what would have happened if we had been together when the German women had called the soldier back. Most likely, we wouldn't have waited for him to arrive and instead would have run, panic-stricken, back to join our group. We might have gotten off with a beating after a failed escape attempt. Decisions hinged on mere seconds then; the two of us would not have had time to hide. Now that my fate had taken a turn for the better – for the time being – my heart was aching to share my good fortune, a nice place to sleep, clean clothes, warm coffee. These emotions would keep on fluctuating according to whether things were going well or badly for me.

I cried myself to sleep, and in the deep stupor brought about by exhaustion and weakness, I slept for exactly twenty-four hours. I only woke up because I heard men talking in the barn. I was gripped by panic. Suddenly I heard someone addressing me in Polish. "Pani! Pani!" [Ma'am!] "I am here," I answered in German. Three men climbed up to join me; two of them were Polish and the third one was introduced to me as a "good" German. I could converse only with the German, who told me that he was a good man and would gladly let me stay in the hayloft, but it was impossible because a lot of Jewish women had escaped the day before while they were passing through the village, and policemen on motorbikes were searching the surrounding villages to round them up. They were paying special attention to barn-like buildings. I had to leave.

I was desperate. I had been feeling so secure to be among good people, and I'd had such a good rest on the bed of hay. Now I had to resume my wandering again. The German instructed me where to go – always in the same direction as the refugees. "No one will notice you in the crowd of people," he said, "but you better wash the blood off your face because that might arouse suspicion."

In the suitcase, perhaps what pleased me the most was the bag of toiletries I found. A comb, a brush and – my God – a small mirror. I had been so tired yesterday that I hadn't taken them out. Now, however, when I looked in the mirror, I had the fright of my life. The last time I had properly looked in a mirror was back at home, and once, in Auschwitz, I had caught a glimpse of myself, bald and in tatters, in a windowpane. That time it had such an awful effect on me, and I only recognized myself because I also saw my ruffled grey cotton dress in the reflection. This time, it was impossible to believe that the person looking back at me was really me.

I saw a haggard little old face with matted greying hair hanging down from under my peaked hood. Half of my face was covered with dried blood. I couldn't see one of my eyes through the blood, while the other half of my face was greyish-black from dirt and the beating. My eye was terribly sore and, near my temple, there was a nasty gash over my eyebrow from which there was still some blood seeping out. And my hand! There was a huge blue welt caused by the blows, the imprint of the truncheon, and a large wound with blood caked over it. I was a horrible sight, and I will never understand how come I was not captured on the highway, looking as scary as I did.

The men gave me water and I began carefully washing my sore eye and my bleeding temple. After a prolonged and miserable session of scraping, the dried up blood was removed and all of a sudden, my eye re-appeared. I could see but oh, what I saw! The little mirror now showed half a face that was changing from dark blue to purple. My eye was closed to a slit and was badly swollen. I looked alarming but at least my face was clean, and the other half had started to resemble something human. I washed my injured hand and bandaged it with a linen kerchief that I had found in the suitcase.

Having tidied myself up, I said goodbye to the Poles, who gave me six large slices of bread with margarine for the road. I made the woman happy with all the children's clothing, and I gave the German the smaller gold chain. He didn't want to accept it, but finally I asked him to accept it in exchange for a few marks, to be able to buy coffee or tea later on. He gave me four marks, which I tied into the corner of my handkerchief and put in the German prayer book I found in the suitcase.

I started out on my trip with a suitcase in one hand – by now considerably lighter – and a prayer book in the other, from which the money knotted up in the handkerchief was bulging out. I became a regular little old woman from the country. Instead of the unmistakable pointed hood, I tied a kerchief around my head.

I set out on my way again with a lighter heart. I didn't go in the direction suggested by the German. I didn't intend to join the ranks of the refugees. No, I headed back toward the Russians. This was easier said than done. As natural as it would have been to flee along with those who were fleeing, it was suspicious to be going in the opposite direction, carrying baggage. On the way, people kept stopping me and asking me where I was going and what had caused the terrible wound and blotches on my face. I offered the following made-up story: I'm a refugee, I fell off the cart that was carrying me, without anyone noticing, and I was left behind on the ground. I'm going back to town to find a doctor who can treat my injuries. They bought the story, and I continued on to Grünberg.

It was a wonderful feeling to walk freely into the town of Grünberg, where I had been watching the passersby and people having their breakfast in the pastry shop with such terrible bitterness a few days before. I strolled along the street, enjoying being able to stop in front of shop windows. I was free! As I was walking toward the town centre on the main street – called Berliner Strasse – I saw cars sitting in a yard located between a large apartment building and a small house. I was very tired and I thought about sitting inside one of them to have a rest. I cautiously made my way into the yard, and among the cars I discovered a beautiful large coach with glass windows. Not too many of those were in use nowadays, so I figured it would not be needed anytime soon. It was a four-seater landau with grey suede upholstery. I sank down on one seat and put my feet up on the seat opposite. I put the suitcase under the seat, covered myself with my blanket and, as always when I found myself in a horizontal position, I fell asleep.

It must have been around noon when I woke up. I ate one slice of the bread with margarine that I'd got from the Poles, and for about an hour I watched from the coach to see what was happening around me. I came to the conclusion that this car storage area was in a dead-end street. There was an old couple living in the little house nearby, perhaps some kind of caretakers. The old man spent a lot of time sweeping. He even swept around my coach while I was hiding down low, trembling, but at last he got tired of it and went inside the house, most likely to have dinner

I carefully got out of the coach, putting the telltale grey blanket under the seat. With the prayer book in my hand, I calmly walked away. I looked at the street name and number to make sure I could find my way back, and I took off to find something to drink. I stopped many women, but no one could answer my question as to where I could get a tea or a coffee. By this point, Grünberg was full of retreating soldiers and refugees and there was a ticket system in place for food. I did not dare to enter a more elegant establishment because of my appearance and besides, I had no idea what I could buy for four marks; my ignorance in this matter might have made me appear suspicious.

Finally, an old man pointed me to a bakery where you could buy coffee. I went in and sat down at a small table and ordered one. I was served ersatz coffee without milk and sugar, but I was badly craving some liquid and drank it voraciously. I asked if I could get a bun and was overjoyed when I was told that in view of the many transients, they had permission to give each person a bun, without a ticket. Two days after having seen it as utterly hopeless that I would ever sit at a table having coffee again, this miracle had happened to me.

As I was happily drinking my coffee and munching on a snow-white crusty bun, a blue-collar worker sat down at my table and started chatting with me. He asked where I was coming from, but I felt too scared to answer. "From far away," I answered cautiously. As to the next inevitable question, I answered vaguely, "I am going wherever my legs will carry me, just like the rest of the refugees."

"How horrible this war is, I wish it was over," he said. "It causes suffering for everyone. That goes for our factory, too, where a thousand young Jewish girls were working. They were so decent, skilled and good. My heart went out to them. I wanted to take one of them home to my family, to save her, but a few days ago they were moved from the factory so the Russians wouldn't find them."

Wisely, I kept quiet, thinking about what I should do. If I revealed my identity, this man would most likely help me. But what if he was an agent provocateur and found me suspicious? I decided not to let him know who I was, and after finishing my breakfast I said goodbye to him. With trepidation, I asked the lady at the cash how much I owed her for breakfast, and I was surprised to hear that it cost a mere twenty-four pfennigs. Everything was so cheap, except you couldn't buy anything without a ticket.

On the way back to the coach I did some calculations that if I lived there and ate such a splendid breakfast every morning, my money would last for two weeks. During that time, something was bound to happen. I still had five slices of bread and margarine left, and I also stashed half of my breakfast bun in my hidden pocket for lunch.

I found my "home," climbed in and made myself comfortable, like I used to do in a fine hotel. I wasn't even cold, since I had my private hot-air heating, warming up the narrow coach with my own breath. I lived in this glassed-in coach for three days, near the main street of Grünberg, right across from the police station. The thought of this adventure often caused me to laugh to myself, and I felt it was a shame that I would never make it home – I was convinced of this – and I would never have a chance to recount my bizarre experience.

I had escaped from my group on Monday and it was already Saturday morning. I was just starting to wake up when someone knocked on the window of my coach. Once again I was gripped by fright, but I tried to conceal it with an air of sang-froid. "Who is in this coach?" a voice asked, the glass door already ajar. The old man, the compulsive sweeper, was standing there. "I'm a poor refugee, I got into town late at night and I didn't have a place to sleep. Don't be upset with me for having spent the night here," I said in a sorrowful tone. "I'm not upset at all," he replied. "Go on and rest at your leisure." He resumed his sweeping. He must have been given a life sentence in sweeping.

I didn't dare stay. What if he summoned a policeman? I told him that I had to leave for the next village where my daughter was waiting for me, and I set out on my way. Now where to go? I came to the conclusion that it was best to go back to the neighbouring village, to the good Polish people. The Germans must have given up on searching for escapees by now, and the Poles would surely hide me in the hayloft.

As I reached the highway, two policemen on motorbikes sped toward me. "Where are you heading?" they asked. "I'm going to my daughter's in the neighbouring village," I replied with a smile. "You mean, to Wittgenau or to the next one, Schweinitz?" "Just here, to Wittgenau," I answered, happy to know at last where I was going and also to know that the second village was called Schweinitz. (That must have been where I escaped from my company.) Wishing me a good trip, they sped off. I kept repeating the names of the villages, which I will never again forget, so I'd be able to say where I was heading in case I was asked.

I went into a German house to ask for water, finding only a young girl there, perhaps about six years old. She thought I was a refugee and asked right away if I was hungry. "I sure am, very much so," I answered. She turned on the single-burner stove and heated up some café au lait for me within seconds. She cut a slice of bread and spread liverwurst on it, and watched me happily while I was feasting. I got a nice, colourful bead necklace out of my suitcase and hung it around her neck. She even gave me a needle and some thread and packed me a slice of bread and liverwurst for the road. Finally, she turned on the radio, which is how I found out that the Soviets were quite close, and Züllichau, where Zsófi had escaped, had long since fallen.

Thanking the little girl for her kindness, I left. As I was sitting on my suitcase by the side of the road taking a rest, two Germans, an older woman and a teenage girl, headed toward me. The girl asked where I was going and I launched into my story. "You're not telling the truth," she said. She had seen me coming and going on the highway for days and could tell by my clothing that I was not German, that I must have escaped from the group of Jewish women who were brought through here.

"Not at all!" I replied, and I took the German prayer book out of my suitcase. This gave her pause, yet she announced that I had to go to Grünberg with her, where I could verify my identity, and if I was Christian, no harm would come to me. There was nothing I could do – I started off toward Grünberg with the two women behind me. Escape was out of the question. There were a lot of people on the road, and those two would have alerted them. My fate has been sealed, I thought. I was not surprised; I would have been surprised if I had succeeded in escaping. Sooner or later my unusual appearance and my Hungarian-sounding German had to arouse suspicion.

In Grünberg, the women handed me over to the traffic policeman standing at the outskirts of town. He asked for my papers, which I didn't have, so he asked the girl to phone for a policeman because he wasn't allowed to leave his post.

When the girl left to make the call, I considered my prospects: I would be handed over to the SS because we were under their jurisdiction, and they would not only kill me – that I had been prepared for, for a long time – but they would torture me first. For some time now, I had not been afraid of death, but my fear of torture and suffering had increased. Why should I go through this? Who knew what had happened to my loved ones? Had my dear deserted daughter managed to flee? And how about my good, sweet husband and my one and only son – were they still alive? Would we ever see each other again?

If I had been rational, I would have answered "no" to all these questions. It was not possible that they had survived atrocities similar to ours or, as we had heard tell, the even more horrific ordeals that the men had to endure. Why should I stay alive? Why bother escaping? What could await me in this life even if, which seemed impossible, I got home? I had lived well, with the world's best husband and gentlest children, in financial security without a problem. I had enjoyed all the happiness life offered. Why should I go on, bitter and alone? I would die; I should put an end to the drama!

These thoughts were spooling through my mind like a movie reel, and when I reached the final conclusion, as if it were a continuation of my thoughts, a huge military vehicle sped toward me. I felt it was my fate rushing at me and, suddenly tearing away from the policeman's grip, I flung myself in front of the speeding car. I heard the screams of the policeman and the bystanders as I waited for death's release. It didn't arrive. The car braked, nudged me a bit on my side, and then stopped. When the policeman rushed over to me, all frightened, and pulled me out from under the front wheels of the car, he must have thought that I had gone mad. I was laughing loudly. I found it so funny that in the past few days I'd almost starved to death, I'd been beaten up, one soldier had wanted to shoot me and another wanted to hang me, and now I was being pulled out from under a car without the slightest injury. I just had to laugh. In that moment, I felt that God still had a purpose for me: I was being sentenced to live.

I decided to leave myself to fate and not attempt suicide again. The policeman who'd been summoned by telephone arrived, and the first one handed me over to him, insisting that he should never let go of my hand because I had a mania for throwing myself under cars. For the third time in my life, I marched into Grünberg. The policeman clutched my arm tightly, followed by the two German women who wanted to make sure that I was indeed taken to the police station, and a crowd of street kids accompanied the interesting procession with glee. She's most likely a Russian spy, was the general consensus of the opinions and guesses put forward as to the probable cause for my arrest.

We didn't go straight to the police station. It was Saturday evening and the shops were about to close, and my policeman, as he confessed while offering apologies, had to buy dinner for his family. Thus we went to four or five shops – the butcher, the dairyman, the baker – hand in hand – to the great delight of the crowd. At last we finished shopping, my mouth watering at the sight of the different goodies, and arrived at the police station. From there we were sent to another one, and then to a third place. I had not been asked who I was or what I was doing. The officers just looked at me, said, "Deutsche Wolle," and then sent me on. I had no idea what Deutsche Wolle meant. Maybe they were referring to my grey woollen blanket?

I didn't know until I found myself in front of the Lager from where we had started off on that Monday morning. Above its gate, I noticed now, was written in large letters, Deutsche Wollwaren. So, it was the name of the textile factory that had given us shelter.

The policeman rang the bell and a German woman opened the gate. "Another new arrival," said the policeman, and he handed me over to the woman, glad to be rid of me and to take home his supper. I was led into the Lager. It was already dark and the doorbell had probably woken the residents. As the door opened, I could hear the sound of inquiring voices speaking, to my greatest joy, in Hungarian! "Where are you coming from? What's your name? Did you escape?" I was inundated with questions. I gave my name, at which point someone jumped off her bed and rushed over to me.

It was Ica, who had shared her pallet with me on our previous night there! It turned out that I was the thirty-sixth escapee who had been caught and brought back to the Lager. Ten of them hadn't even left the place; instead they had hidden in the upper bunks, and the German woman found them the next day. She doled out a few slaps on the face, but nothing else happened to them. If only I hadn't left that time with Ági... but back then this possibility had never even occurred to me.

There was great rejoicing, and I relayed to them how I had escaped and all that I had lived through since. They brought me a fine supper of creamed potatoes, but I was so scared that the heavy food would do damage to my empty stomach that I hardly ate anything. I enjoyed all the more the sugary coffee, of which I could get as much as I wanted. I drank about a litre of it.

When I was captured, I had been prepared for everything except for being given a splendid dinner among friends and sleeping in a fine bed complete with white linens. My tumultuous life had reached a place of respite. When I thought of that mean young woman who reported me I actually felt grateful. I got into bed and then Ica and the others started to tell their escape stories. Of course, each story was essentially the same, but with slight variations. Escape was near impossible; it might have taken days or weeks, but eventually everyone was captured.

Ica had escaped right in Grünberg, with three of her friends, when we first started off. They leapt through a doorway. When the woman who lived in that house spotted them, she locked the door with a key to prevent the soldiers from following them, hid them all in the cellar, and cooked some soup for them. She kept them there until the evening and then sent them on their way because she was afraid that when the other tenants of the building returned, they would find them, and that could cost her her life. She described which way to go to reach the nearest village, from which the German population had already fled, and advised them to take shelter in an empty house until the Soviets arrived. She even gave them food for the road. There were many people like her among the Germans.

The next day, the German woman suggested that I stay in bed because I looked awful. We received nourishing food – after all, their storage room was full – sweet coffee, creamed vegetables that tasted like at home, cabbage, carrots. When we got roast pork with pickles and potatoes, followed by sweet macaroni, for our Sunday dinner, I thought it must be a dream. God, if only Ági could be here as well! That was all I could think of.

The wound on my hand had gotten infected. Of course, I hadn't been able to treat it during my wanderings, not that I had anything to treat it with. My whole hand was a horrible, open wound, oozing blood and pus, and the pain went all the way to my elbow. At last my hand was bandaged, but the putrid pus seeped through the dressing immediately, and that almost made the person who bandaged it sick.

As the days passed, we were treated so well that we could not imagine what they intended to do with us. We figured it was out of the question to be kept there for a long time and be fed without having to work. The ten women who had stayed in hiding in the Lager were being cared for by Red Cross nurses. One girl had broken her leg when she tried to jump down from the bed; the leg was put in a cast and she was given proper care. We were fed very well, and amply. No one was required to work, except to keep the Lager tidy, and I stayed in bed for eight days on a fattening-up diet, in the strict sense of the word. I felt so sad about Ági.

New escapees were brought in every day but no one arrived from our group. I had no news of Ági. One woman did mention that she had marched with her to Christianstadt, where they rested in a Lager. They were fed and given bread for the road, but that is where the woman escaped so she didn't know anything further. I couldn't get it out of my mind for a second, what might have become of Ági. It was an awful feeling, that while I was trying to save her from staying behind because of me, I was actually the one who escaped. Now I was doing exceedingly well and she continued to starve. That was on my mind with every bite I took and my heart almost broke from longing for her. She hadn't dared to follow me because she didn't possess the same deadly determination that I did – I, who didn't care at all whether I was shot this day or the next, for it was to be my fate, regardless. Ági wanted to live and she didn't dare risk being caught after an escape and being shot for it. After all, the only reason I was saved was that the henchman with the Hitler moustache believed I was dead.

I kept wondering why, now, the Germans were behaving so decently all of a sudden, giving us food. It was suspicious how abruptly they had become so generous, and we surmised this meant that the Soviets were near. Otherwise, there was no other sign that our saviours were approaching.

I made friends with my companions, and eight of us stuck together – eight completely different people who were bound together only by a common fate and a common interest. I was the oldest among them and they treated me with kindness. They felt sorry for the terrible state my hand was in and washed me, combed my hair, brought me my meals in bed. It certainly felt good after having suffered neglect for so long. Mrs. Marcsa Zimmermann from Várad took especially good care of me.

There was a lot of clothing left in the Lager that had belonged to the factory workers, which we could select from to dress ourselves quite properly. We managed to get rid of the lice at last. We could bathe and we could wash our clothes. We then realized that, even in captivity, not everyone was as badly treated as we had been. The close to one thousand young women who had worked in this factory had lived like human beings. They had decent clothes, underwear, could bathe and most likely received better food as well. In the lockers we found cosmetics and even the cologne we'd been so badly missing.

I had been in the Lager for nine days when I was finally strong enough to get out of bed and get dressed in the nice clothes I'd been given. It was Sunday again, and we were chatting amiably and sitting around the stove, doing some darning. What would become of us? How long were they going to keep us here? One of the girls told us that her German friend who worked in the factory was going to help her to escape and take her to his family. I wondered if this was the worker who'd had the conversation with me in the coffee shop.

All of a sudden, the door burst open and the woman soldier entered in a state of agitation. "Pack up and get dressed," she said, "we are taking you away from here!" This gave us an awful scare. The girl who had just been talking about her escape broke into loud sobs. The sick people who couldn't get onto their feet were crying. I consoled them, but without much conviction, as I was sure they'd be shot. We packed and got dressed in deathly silence; all you could hear was the beating of our hearts.

The German woman left. By now I had a lot of stuff to pack, and the little blue suitcase, my faithful companion, was full of clothes and food. We got ready and waited. We waited for hours, but the German woman didn't come back. I had enough of waiting and resolved not to start the march all over again, and to flee instead. I saw that a few Polish girls had the same idea. The Hungarian women had already disappeared. Not a single one was in sight. Only the sick people were lying in their beds, scared to death.

The Polish women pushed open the door and rushed out to the yard, cut a hole in the wire fence and slipped through it. I followed them. We were ready to face the world. But the young women walked faster than I did, I lagged behind, and there I was, trudging along the highway all by myself. I was walking and walking with no idea whether I was headed in the right direction. I had never been to this part of the town and I didn't know my way.

At last I reached a village. A woman was standing in the doorway of the first house and she asked me where I was headed. "I am a refugee," I said. "I am fleeing from the Russians." "That sounds suspicious," the woman said, "because we are fleeing too, but in the opposite direction." "Then I must have gotten lost," I replied. I turned around in haste and started back the other way.

By now I could tell that Grünberg would be my destiny because no matter which direction I set out, I always arrived back there. I decided to return to the Lager to see what had happened to the others, except I couldn't find my way back. We had cut the fence somewhere behind the Lager, we had reached the highway through a vineyard, and I didn't know which way to go. I kept walking until it turned into evening. On the outskirts of Grünberg, I saw an open shed where planks were stored. There was no one around and I went into the dark room. I scarcely had time to look around when I heard someone approaching. A light shone into the room, right in my face. "I'm a refugee looking for shelter," I said calmly. "Go ahead and lie down," a man's voice said. "You can use the sacks in the corner to cover yourself." Thanking him, I grabbed a couple sacks and lay down on a narrow plank.

I was woken by the cold. It was morning and I was completely covered by the snow that had been falling all night. I looked like a snow-laden grave, and I could hardly climb out from under it. Fortunately, the sacks had protected my clothes from getting wet. I set out again on my pilgrimage. I had food, for we had gathered all we could from the Lager's kitchen.

I was trudging along the streets of Grünberg, in a completely un-familiar part of town, when a woman stopped and spoke to me. Her looks inspired trust, and at her questioning I told her that I was a prison worker from a Lager, had been left behind by the Germans because I was sick, and did not know where to go. "I'm Polish and I will gladly help you," she said. She explained which way to go to reach a Lager where Polish and French gentiles were living. "They will be glad to welcome you and give you food. It is the workers' Lager of a munitions factory."

I managed to find the Lager, which was quite far. I went straight into the cafeteria and saw about fifty people, both men and women, sitting in a room, with a lot of bundles. I sat down beside the stove to warm up and dry my clothes, which had gotten wet from the con-tinuously falling snow. An older woman turned to me and offered bread. We started talking in German, and she told me that all those around us were Russian, Ukrainian or Polish prisoners, waiting for the Germans to transport them away from the advancing Soviets. "They must be near if they aren't letting us stay here any longer," said the friendly woman.

A short while later a cart arrived; they loaded their belongings on to it and the people followed after it on foot. I was by myself. I knocked on the door of a barracks, where the capital letter "F" in-dicated that the occupants were French. I found three women there, and since I spoke French, they gave me a warm welcome. Half the face and body of one of them, a Belgian, had been burnt in an explo-sion in the munitions factory where they worked. This once beautiful young woman was now a terrible sight.

In answer to my question of whether I could stay in their place, I was told that only the French could live in this barracks. The Germans carried out frequent surprise inspections, so they couldn't take the risk of having a stranger found in their midst. On the other hand, the Lager was full of rooms vacated by the Russians, Poles and Ukrainians who had just been transported away, and I should feel free to enter any of them. I walked through all the barracks and found a small empty room outfitted with a bed, a locker and a flat-topped stove. I moved in with my battered suitcase, made a fire, put some potatoes on to cook and made myself at home.

In each room I found food that had been left behind, so food was not an issue. I lived in this small room for three days. On the third night, the walls of the barracks were shaken by a tremendous bombardment. In the past days we had heard shelling nearby, so I didn't think much of it, but the present shelling was unusually strong and frequent. Our saviours – the Soviets – must be nearby after all, I thought happily.

Freedom

On the morning of February 15, I opened the window and saw a hustle and bustle in the yard. The occupants of the Lager were coming and going, dressed and carrying parcels. One of the women shouted over to me to come along with her to Grünberg, that there were clothes, shoes, and food lying in the street.

"Why? What has happened?" I asked in surprise.

"Don't you know? The Russians marched into Grünberg last night!"

I had never felt such joy before. I threw myself onto my bed, sobbing, and I could barely calm myself enough to go into town. For the fifth time, this time, for the last time, I walked into Grünberg. What a different sight the town was now. The stuck-up German women with the ever-present shopping bags in their hands, the proud policemen, the retreating soldiers, had all disappeared from the streets. The shops had been broken into, the windows of all the houses had been shot out and the doors were agape.

I entered one of these ransacked houses. The rooms hadn't been touched but the contents of the wardrobes were scattered in the middle of the room – the same way I had found my apartment when the Germans were finished with it. I must say, it felt good to see a swastika-adorned home all vandalized, after what had been done to us. It was a joy to know that the proud, cruel Germans who had made millions of people homeless were rendered homeless themselves. It was a joy to search through the belongings they'd left behind, to see the traces of their hasty flight, and to know that most likely their hearts had ached when they had to leave their homes, the same way it had hurt us when we had had to tie up the fruits of a life's labour into a single bundle to take along with us. This gave me no small satisfaction.

I moved into this empty house. There was plenty of food. You could find a lot of flour, sugar and hundreds of preserves in each house. It wasn't for nothing that they had robbed all of Europe; they had been amply provided for. Even during peacetime we'd never had snow-white bread like the Germans were eating in the seventh year of the war. The only thing they lacked was lard.

I was curious to learn what had happened to my comrades, and I took off to find the Deutsche Wolle Lager. Then, I saw all my Hungarian friends from the Lager coming from the opposite direction, carrying the sick on stretchers. After the mutual flood of questions, I managed to find out that my flight had been unnecessary because it was the Germans who had fled from us! The woman soldier never returned to the Deutsche Wolle. It seems their flight was so urgent that they didn't have time to bother with us and left us to our fate. The women all hid in the attic and dared to come out only the next day. They were locked in, but the Germans had disappeared.

This had always been our dream. Back in Auschwitz we'd been dreaming that one day we'd wake up with the guards gone from in front of the door and we'd be free. This miracle had happened to them! They had broken into the storage room and for two days they kept cooking and baking. On the third day, someone rattled the door. Only Ica was close by, the rest were busy in the kitchen, and since the door was locked from the outside, she couldn't open it. The impatient rattler finally switched to more effective means and broke down the door with a swift kick. To Ica's great astonishment, there was a soldier standing in front of her with a red star on his cap.

"Nemetski!" (German!) the soldier shouted, and pointed his machine gun right at her. Ica, on the other hand, rushed up to the shocked soldier, pushed the machine gun aside, flung herself at him, embraced him and kissed him. He was dumbstruck by this unexpected counter-offensive, and then Ica turned and ran to the kitchen, screaming, "The Russians are here!"

The other women cast pitying glances at one another. "She must have lost her mind, the poor thing." "It's all right, it's all right," they all said, "just sit down here," and they insisted on having her drink some water to bring her back to her senses.

"Truly," Ica protested loudly, "there is a Russian soldier here. There's a red star on his cap and he wanted to shoot me!" They tried to calm her down, but by then the Russian soldier had appeared in the doorway and shot off a series of questions as to who they were. Then the whole bunch of them rushed at him, hugging and kissing him, crying and laughing. One of them who knew Slovak explained to him that they were prisoners and that he was the one who had freed them. At this point, the soldier suddenly seemed very proud of himself. He sat down to chat with them; he ate, he drank, he offered them some of his food, and then he left.

My friends had worried about me a lot and couldn't imagine what might have happened to me. By the time they wanted to alert me to go into hiding with them in the attic, I had disappeared. They told me that they were on their way to a sanatorium, to leave the sick people there. What a strange sight the procession must have made. In the front, the sick were carried on stretchers. Behind them came Ica, dragging the corpse of a huge turkey a soldier had shot for them. Two of them were carrying half a pig from the same source.

I joined the group and, after leaving the sick behind in the sanatorium, we headed off to the Lager. We cooked turkey soup, pork chops, stuffed cabbage. The clouds were dispersing at last in our overcast sky, and the long-awaited red star had appeared in it, bringing freedom. Relli, one of our companions from Kassa, a very active, capable woman who spoke Slovak, had stayed behind in town, and she arrived for dinner with some Polish men, gentile prisoners. "I have decided," she said, "to start off for home, and whoever wants to can join me."

I looked at her as if she'd gone mad. To go home had been such an unattainable dream for eight months, that now that someone mentioned it as a possibility it sounded like a joke. "Just how do you propose to do it?" I asked. "You want us to set out without money or papers, without a railway?" "Yes," she said. "Come if you want, and if not, I'll still go with the Poles." She was so self-confident and decisive that she convinced us; besides, she was the only one among us who knew a Slavic language. In no time, we decided to go with her. Right away we roasted the entire half pig and cooked more of the turkey for the road. We loaded our bundles onto small carts that were actually toy wagons that children used to pull each other around. We found one of these in every house.

Three days after being liberated, on February 18, we started off on our journey. Our guide and protector during the whole trip was an old saddler from Warsaw. By evening, we reached a village. We heard a cow mooing near one of the houses. It looked to be a handsomely furnished village house. "Let's go in there," I suggested. The Pole milked the cow and we made coffee to go with some of the thirty kilos of sugar we'd brought along. We ate a fine supper, and in the morning we continued on our way. By now, I could walk easily. I'd found a pair of splendid, light high-top boots, made of kid leather, in my "apartment." It was a pleasure to walk in a pair of new women's shoes after the size forty-two men's boots that had chafed my feet.

However, our next place to take a rest, Neusalz, by the Oder, was still far away. Fortunately, after we had walked about ten kilometres, some Italian prisoners on two carts caught up to us. They stopped when we waved at them, let us climb on board, tied our wagons to the carts and pulled them along behind.

I kept saying that I was afraid it was not going to be so easy to cross the Oder, given that there was most likely no bridge. All the bridges had been blown up by the retreating Germans, and naturally that was the case here as well. As we reached the riverbank, some men halted our carts. We women stayed cautiously behind, waiting to see what would happen to our Italians. Indeed, their carts were confiscated, and they were taken away to do bridge building.

We turned right around and rushed back to the town, our wagons behind us, not even waving goodbye to the poor friendly Italians. Where we should spend the night was our next problem. As we were discussing, I noticed a Frenchman with a red armband, and turned to him for advice. He said he knew of a good place and I should go with him. He led us to the yard of a blown-up gas factory, which was lying in ruins on the outside, but the workers' quarters in the yard were completely unscathed. One of these apartments was occupied by a Yugoslavian partisan friend of his, Franz, who had been a forced labourer in the gas factory.

I will never forget the cordial welcome that our host gave us. He was living on the ground floor of the house and he let us take the first floor. This German style of building is quite interesting. Every house has two storeys with an interior oak staircase leading to the upper storey, which in reality was the loft. This particular apartment had belonged to a locksmith. Back home, only the well-to-do bourgeois people had such accommodations. Splendid kitchens in each house, walls tiled all around, linoleum flooring, built-in cupboards equipped with the best household items. Each kitchen had an excellent stove that operated on coal, gas or electricity. This was the norm everywhere in the villages and farmhouses where we paid our respects along the way.

We had a fine apartment and great beds with snow-white linen. We began housekeeping in earnest. Ica and a friend from Várad did the cooking, two young women from Tasnád did the cleaning, and the rest of us went on search missions to neighbouring houses. The town was empty; only about a hundred old folks had stayed behind. The apartments were awaiting our visits with open doors. Of course, all of them had been searched through before, but we still managed to find a lot of food and plenty of clothes. Éva, a charming friend from Vienna, and Muci Balázsfalvy, a dancer from Pest, were the most successful at the searching mission. They found a lot of flour, sugar and other food such as preserves and bacon in each house. There were triumphant cries when they rolled in a little barrel of sauerkraut.

At last we could enjoy the tastes of home. We fulfilled all our desires by cooking and baking all the dishes we had been talking about with such longing when we were digging ditches. Potato *lángos*, fried dough! Plum butter *derelye*, jam pockets! With each bite, all I could think of was Ági. How happily she would eat these treats, and how she must be starving.

I couldn't do much, given the terrible state of my hands. On the third day after our arrival, Franz took me to see an old German doctor. He had stayed at home with his daughter. No harm had befallen the men who remained in the town but the women, unfortunately, were at the mercy of the Soviet soldiers. The doctor examined my hand and was practically horrified. The joints, veins, sinews, naked, without skin, looked like the frightening illustrations in a medical book. Bloody pus was gushing out and I couldn't move my forefinger at all.

I never would have believed that one day skin would form again on my hand, for my weakened, vitamin-depleted body did not contain any regenerative material. The doctor cleaned my hand, sprinkled some powder on the wound, bandaged it, and warned me to let him know right away if the pain in my arm reached the shoulder, because in that case my hand would need to be amputated to save my life. So far, the pain reached only my elbow. Thanks to the old doctor, who treated my wound with the utmost care every day, the pain ceased and the wound started to get smaller. The treatment and proper nourishment had started the healing process, and the wound eventually completely healed, though my finger remained paralyzed forever.

~

Relli, the forever restless one of our group, kept roaming the streets, trying to make connections with people who might help us to get home. One time, she returned from her reconnaissance mission with a Czech guy. He was a butcher in a neighbouring village and he wanted to go home with us as well. He provided us with meat, and he had a cart and even a horse, on which he offered to transport us. However, there was no hope of that for the time being. The bridge was not finished and it seemed that we were going to stay in Neusalz for months. We already knew all the inhabitants of the little town, and we felt quite at home. The seemingly inexhaustible food supply had a reassuring effect on our mood.

On one occasion, an old Russian soldier happened to enter our place. Up to then, no one had discovered our quarters in the ruined gas factory. We found a lot of wine in the cellars and treated our guest in style. Right away he started courting Relli, who was the only one who could talk to him, but she was not too fazed by it because we figured the polite visitor, whose name was Gusko Konstantinovich, was about sixty. He had only one tooth, but he kept showing it all the time because it protruded from his mouth, giving a friendly, grinning expression to his scruffy face. Our Russian had a few drinks, and then he left.

In the evening, we were having supper when our Gusko showed up again, but this time he was not alone. The soldier who came with him had one eye swollen shut, which gave his face a mischievous look, and used his other eye to cast bewitching glances at the beautiful Éva. He introduced himself as a cook and to prove it he produced a huge piece of bacon that he handed over to Éva as if it were a delicate flower. Éva, having a rather materialistic nature, immediately grew animated. She started a friendly exchange in sign language with the Russian, at which point a few canned goods also surfaced from his pocket. He set them down on our table and started drinking diligently with our Pole, who was always willing to sacrifice himself. The Russian demanded that we also drink along with them and not only that, but that we drink from his glass, most likely to conform to some Russian rules of etiquette.

Our friend Gusko was wooing Relli and kept visiting us. Sometimes he would arrive at midnight, which seemed to us a somewhat unusual time for a visit, but my goodness, other lands, other customs! Nothing surprised us any more. We teased Relli about her elderly suitor, but he proved to be rather useful. Relli told him that we had only one horse and we needed one more. Next day, Gusko Konstantinovich led a stalwart steed right into our kitchen. When the mare was harnessed together with our little pony-like horse, they formed such a comical ensemble that we burst out laughing. However, we showered Gusko with our heartfelt thanks. We drank from his glass – let him see that we knew how it was done! – and the ladies who smoked smiled at him gratefully when he rolled a cigarette for them, licked it to seal it, lit it, then slipped it between their lips.

"How old are you?" I asked him once. "Twenty-eight," he answered, to our great astonishment. Well, if we had bugged Relli about an old suitor before, now we teased her even more about a young one. "He could be your son!" we said to pretty and young-looking Relli, who was forty-two years old. We carried on like this even though we all owed a huge debt of gratitude to Relli. I don't know how we would have gotten home without her. She kept visiting the Russian headquarters, but for the time being they were not issuing travel permits.

We had been in Neusalz for more than three weeks. We had each put on about ten pounds, were dressing nicely and starting to look like human beings again. Éva, who had been an English teacher in Vienna, found a suitor who was a hairdresser from Paris. He was allowed to receive care packages from home and kept bringing her even better food. We had everything and we were not in a great hurry to leave and face uncertainty.

Relli visited the headquarters relentlessly until one day she brought the news, waving the permit triumphantly, that there was no obstacle to our departure anymore. We were elated and then again, we were not. After all, who knew what lay in store for us? Would we come across such a pleasant, friendly home again during our wanderings?

Our old Pole readied the cart and horses for our departure. He lined the carts with red blankets in honour of the Russians and harnessed David and Goliath, the names I had given to these two steeds of very different sizes.

The day of our departure arrived: we set out on March 15, under the banner of freedom.[2] We said goodbye to friendly little Neusalz, the only place in Germany that I recall with fondness. Everyone brought along some souvenirs. Muci, the dancer from Pest, took a few silver artifacts and etchings depicting the town, from the local museum. We all carried with us some silverware, bedding, pots and pans, so as not to be in need of anything whenever we stopped along the way.

We climbed up onto the cart, on top of the many parcels. Our Yugoslavian host had grown so fond of us that he set out for home with us as well. He drove the horses while the old Pole walked beside the cart. Our procession looked as funny as a travelling circus. We reached the Oder and were allowed to cross on the newly finished bridge. We were relieved, but we weren't certain which way to go, so we proceeded in whatever direction the thousands and thousands of refugees were taking. There were masses of liberated prisoners, on carts, on foot, on bicycles, going in one direction, while from the other came the Soviet soldiers in an endless flood. We waved at them happily. After all, we owed it to them that we had been freed from Hitler's cursed captivity.

All along the way we passed the stinking corpses of animals that had starved to death, and a hungry goat followed us for hours hoping for some food. At first, our butcher was quite willing to turn it into a meal, but then he declared that the poor thing was so skinny it was

---

2 Refers to March 15, 1848, the first day of the Hungarian Freedom Fight of 1848–49.

useless to kill it; it would soon die on its own. By evening, we arrived in a village.

We got down off the cart to look for shelter for the night. A horrible scene confronted us. The village we arrived at appeared to be cursed. Not a living soul anywhere, only hundreds of dead animals on the road, in the yard, even in the rooms. The houses were in such terrible condition that it was impossible to enter any of them. The rooms were ransacked and soiled, the furniture, mirrors and windows broken. In one house, we came across the corpses of three women. This was enough to dissuade us from entering any more houses, and so, after the soft beds in Neusalz, we returned to our old love – straw.

Each village we passed was empty, the site of awful destruction and devastation. By the roadside, hundreds of broken-down cars, prams whose wheels had fallen off, horses with their innards show-ing, cows starting to decay, a horrendous sweet stench emanating from them. All this marked the path of war.

This is what Germany had become. This was the consequence of Hitler's despicable politics. And we, on whom the Nazi henchmen had unleashed a sea of suffering and a flood of pain, saw it with sat-isfaction. Yes! Let them find out what it means to be homeless, to wander around like paupers with crying children in their arms, even though they had not been condemned to death the way our little ones, our old and weak had been. No amount of atonement would suffice for their sins.

On the third day, we arrived at the edge of a town, greatly surprised when we saw the name Schlesiersee on the sign! After two months, we had made it back to the place from which starved, shadow-like women and freezing, crying, moaning, and wailing sick people in wheelbarrows had been sent on their way that miserable night.

We could now walk around freely in the lovely lakeside town, whose coveted, beautiful, peaceful houses were standing there with their doors open. We could enter the plundered, wrecked, soiled houses. Where had the happy families, the laughing children, vanished to? They had been swept away by the winds of war that had blown us so far away from our country, our family, our home.

We continued on toward the Polish border, which was not too far anymore. On our way, however, we saw the ditches we had dug. They were intact; the Germans had not gotten use out of our labour and we hadn't harmed the Russians. We had never believed for a moment that our work was necessary. Like everything else, it had been invented simply to torture us.

It was around noon when we emerged from a forest and caught sight of the boundary stone with Poland written on it. We happily crossed the border out of hated Germany, and it was only at this point that we felt really free.

Soon, the outlines of the first Polish village were visible. When we arrived there, we rode up to the first house and our old Pole kissed the ground of his country, sobbing. The owners came out to see us, embraced their compatriot, who had been through so much, and welcomed us all warmly into their house. We rested at their place for a few days while they fed us, gave us drinks and provisioned us with everything, including food, for the road. On March 21, 1945, the first day of spring, we set out for home with cheerful hearts, toward Freedom.

Our host accompanied us to the first railway station, where we gave him our cart and horses and everything we wouldn't need on the train in exchange for his kind hospitality. We succeeded in catching a train that was about to leave, and at last, not on foot, not on a cart, but on a real train, we were moving, not swiftly, but bumping along toward home. After that, we travelled in various ways – passenger cars, cattle cars, together with horses, sleeping on a pile of coal – until we reached Krakow.

Our first stop was the public baths, the second was the pastry shop. We sold everything that we could, and we sat and ate pastries all day. This was the first time we had seen real sweets in a whole year. Real chocolate pastries with whipped cream, like in peacetime.

It was worth it to have survived all the suffering, was our unanimous conclusion.

In Krakow, five of our companions took their leave. The rest of us, Relli, Ica and I, decided to rest up properly. We sat in the town park and repeated out loud, "We are free! We are free! We are going home!" Otherwise we wouldn't have believed that it was true. Only someone who has had to live surrounded by electrified fences, who has had to fear every moment that the whim of man could send her to the crematorium, knows what freedom means. Only that person who could have been struck by the stick of Grese, the angel-faced devil, can truly enjoy freedom.

For three days, we indulged in the joys of resting, bathing and eating in the beautiful old city of Krakow, and then we set out. On the train, we made the acquaintance of three officers from Belgrade, royal guards who had been Hitler's prisoners for three years. They relieved us of all the worries of travel. They found us shelter for the night, prepared excellent breakfasts and dinners, made divine American hot chocolate, and carried our parcels. When they got off the train in Nagymihály, together with Relli, they said goodbye by kissing our hands, and Ica, who was the only one left with me, started crying. "I feel like a human being again," she said. I looked at her in surprise because I had never felt any other way. If someone hurt me, I considered it as if I had been kicked by a horse on the street, or bitten by a dog. Only by viewing it with detachment had it been possible to endure the tremendous suffering and humiliation; not for a moment had I considered myself less than before, back home.

The train was carrying us towards Csap, where I was to say goodbye to Ica. The closer we came to home, the more our hearts clenched. Up to this point we would have liked to push the slowly advancing train forward, but now we would have liked to hold it back. What, and more importantly, whom would we find at home? Did we have a home at all, a place where we could lay our heads? Painful questions, to which there were no answers.

I was aware that none of my loved ones could be home yet. We must have been among the first to set out for home. I did not want to arrive alone, back at the place from which eleven of us had set out on our sad, deathly journey. Ica was crying so hard, saying over and over that she didn't dare to go home, that I took pity on her and invited her to come with me. But, as fate would have it, it was not Ica who came with me to Szatmár but I who went to Nyíregyháza with her. For when we arrived at Csap, I had just missed the train and the next one was not due for three days. The train to Nyíregyháza departed the next day, and so we ended up clambering aboard that one, and we two scraggly wayfarers, who had endured so much, arrived at Nyíregyháza on Easter Sunday.

Ica found her brother-in-law, the lawyer, there, so she had a home where she was received with joy. I found my nephew, Gyuri Geiger, who had returned from the Ukraine, and so I spent Easter in the bosom of family, sitting around a table covered with a white cloth.

On Tuesday, April 3, at night, my train pulled into Szatmár.

I clutched my heart because I felt it was going to jump out of my chest, whether from joy or sorrow, I couldn't tell.

I was home, but alone. I had come back, but for what? How would my native town, which had denied me and driven me away, receive me? Plagued by such doubts, I arrived at the Home of the Deportees in Szatmár. They welcomed me. Breakfast and a warm bath awaited each deportee. Only a few had made it back so far. I was among the very first. I wondered how many long months this nice institution would be needed before all those who had survived would return.

Feeling refreshed, I headed into the city. After seeing the railway station, which was almost pulverized by shelling, and the many houses lying in ruins, I saw with great surprise that, albeit somewhat damaged, our house was still standing! All of a sudden, who should rush over to me but my sweet friend Gizi, who had stood by our side so selflessly during the terrible days of our trials. We kissed each other, crying and laughing at the same time, and she led me to her home, which has remained my home to this day, and thus I have not experienced the awful loneliness that I had dreaded during the whole trip. May God bless her for it.

At the news of my arrival, my siblings – Lászlo, Iren and Ödön – who had been living in Romania and had luckily survived, hurried to come and see me, and what bliss it was to be together with my family again! When my dear little daughter was separated from me and I was wandering by myself among foreign people in a foreign land, I had often experienced the bitterness of loneliness, of not belonging to anyone.

Waiting

I have come to the end of my exploits. I have been at home for weeks and I am trying to rebuild our new life, our new nest, from the ruins. By the time my loved ones – God willing – come back, a warm home will be waiting for them, where we will try to forget the horrors we have endured and will try to heal each other's painful wounds.

On May 31, 1945, the anniversary of the departure of the last train of deportees from Szatmár, the local Jews held a memorial service. Young men who had escaped deportation to death camps by working in labour camps, and young women who had somehow weathered this terrible year, constitute the Jewry of Szatmár today, along with a few elderly men and women whose escape is nothing short of a miracle.

This handful of Jews held the memorial service in the little, old temple. The heart-wrenching song for the dead sounded and the loud wailing shook even its stone walls. After all, this song for the dead was for tens and tens of thousands.

All those who had been incinerated. All those who had been killed. All those who had been buried without a song and all those who had not even been buried, just left to die by the roadside.

Everybody was mourning. There were many who were the only survivors of a large family, but there were even more families who had perished without any survivor to weep for them. No more parents, no more children. No spouses for those who return. We were crying, sobbing, and our petrified hearts were a bit relieved.

Then we walked through the ghetto, the site of so many bitter memories. It was lying in ruins and maybe that's a good thing. Let all trace of this mark of shame of the twentieth century disappear. The sad remembrance of it will never disappear from our hearts anyway. The crowded streets of last year are eerily quiet. The gapingly empty – so cramped last year – houses tell the stories of what they have lived through. Where have their occupants gone? Where are the laughing children who sweetened the bitterness of the ghetto? Our old people, whose every step we watched over? The fine young mothers, the new martyrs, who died the fiery death because of their little ones? Who will answer for all those who perished because of the insane ideas of a madman? Who will replace the irreplaceable? Who will heal the un-healable wounds of our hearts?

We also marched to the cemetery to bewail our sorrows to our long-departed loved ones, to whom God had been merciful, and who had found eternal rest where they had lived, loved and suffered – and not on the fields of Auschwitz, where the spring wind would carry, sweep and scatter their ashes, to the eternal shame of those who had brought this about, and to the eternal sorrow of those who survived, who would not forget until their dying day.

~

Six months have passed since I arrived home. Six months full of hope, waiting, heart-gripping anxiety and dark despair. With fear and trepidation, I asked everyone who returned whether they knew anything of my people. At last, an acquaintance brought good news. On his way home, he had met my husband and son, who had endured the trials of the terrible year, were liberated, and once they had recovered their strength somewhat, they were to leave for home too.

With unspeakable joy and with an ecstatic heart, I waited for them for weeks. But the weeks kept passing and so did the months, and all I had endured up to that point paled in comparison with what I lived through during this time. They were not coming, and I walked in a daze to meet each arriving train with more and more anxiety and less and less hope. I waited together with the others who, with their hands clutching their hearts, the excitement of expectation on their pale, weary faces, and a glimmer of hope in their eyes, were staring like lunatics at the face of each person getting off the train. Maybe one of these wavering shadows leaving the train with timid, unsteady steps and a faraway gaze, and with a wan, painful smile, closer to tears, on his virtually unrecognizable yellow face, maybe he could be the hoped-for one?

After two months of awful expectation, the day came when my son, János, got off the train. Alone. I didn't need to ask anything. I took one look at his grief-stricken eyes and despondent face and I knew the terrible truth. While my heart was overflowing with happiness to hold my son in my arms again, enjoying his surprised glee on finding me home alive, part of my heart was suffering for my dear husband.

We were rejoicing over each other and didn't talk about anything else until that evening, in the soft white bed, János burst out crying. He was lamenting his father, who would have liked so much to rest one more time in a white bed in a tidy home, who had desired so badly to be together with us and who didn't live to experience this day. I cried along with him, and it took hours before he calmed down enough to be able to relate the details of our tragedy.

From Auschwitz they went to Brieg, Germany, where they were treated relatively well because my husband was in charge of the construction of the Lager. This didn't last long. They were next taken to Gross-Rosen concentration camp, where they suffered terribly, then were transferred to a subcamp of Gross-Rosen called Langenbielau, where they did very hard work in a factory. After they had been there for five months, they were in a completely debilitated state. All those unable to work were loaded onto carts, thinking that they were going to be taken to a crematorium, and instead were transported to a hospital in a subcamp called Dörnhau. Here people kept dying of starvation, and they would have met the same fate had they not run into Ernő Rosner from Bikszád, who was the cook and storeroom manager there. He led them to his own room, fed them and fattened them up, and did everything in his power to help them regain strength. This decent man helped not only them, but many other acquaintances as well. Thus they were in reasonable physical condition when, one May morning, they woke up to discover that all the SS guards had fled and they were free.

What happiness! They had lived to see the end, the total defeat of the Germans, and they could leave for home. My husband, however, felt too weak to travel so they moved into a German house to recuperate. They set out one week later. They crossed the Riesengebirge Mountains, the border between Poland and Czechoslovakia, on foot, together with Andris, the son of Endre Wohl, our landlord in the ghetto – the eight-times decorated colonel who died of starvation in Dörnhau right before their eyes.

It was my husband who best withstood the rigours of walking, it was he who encouraged the boys to persevere, and they did manage to reach the railway station, where they got on a train leaving for Brünn, but before reaching Brünn, all three of them came down with a high fever, and so they got off the train in a small town and checked into the hospital. They were immediately diagnosed with typhus. They had contracted the infection in Dörnhau from typhus patients brought into their Lager five days before their liberation.

All three of them were lying there, unconscious, for two weeks. One morning, János woke up to discover that his father was not beside him. Frightened and deathly weak, he started looking for him and found him in the corridor, covered with a grey blanket, dead. It was János who closed his father's blessed eyes.

With their youthful metabolism, the boys had managed to beat the high fever even in their weakened state, but my dear husband, who had longed so much for a happy reunion, which he had every reason to hope for, lost the battle. His generous heart, tortured and weakened by worry, hard labour, starvation and the rough treatment of his superiors – a heart that had beat only for everything beautiful, noble and good – stopped forever.

On May 31, the anniversary of our deportation and the day on which we held such a moving commemorative service in Szatmár, my dear, true, life companion, the best man ever, was buried in Ústí nad Orlicí, in the Czech land, at the age of fifty. The better half of my life lies in an unmarked grave.

And my sweet, only little daughter, Ágnes, has not returned home yet either. Our friend Magda Schönberger from Nagyvárad brought the latest news about her. Magda escaped at the end of March, in terrible condition, which meant she had stayed with Ági for five more weeks after my escape. How was my daughter able to walk that long? A divine miracle! When I stayed behind in the German house, Ági wanted to escape as well, in the same village, which is what I also hoped for. Magda told me that it got more and more difficult to escape, and whoever was caught was immediately shot, and although the poor thing tried to stay behind when she saw that I wasn't coming out of the German house, she didn't dare to risk it herself.

On March 2, Ági, Herta and Magda's sister and sister-in-law, together with three hundred others, got selected, partially because they could no longer walk, and partially because they didn't have any shoes, and they were put on a train and given the explanation that they were being sent to the same destination that those on foot would reach only two days later. According to Magda, by that time the weak were not being killed any more and moreover, they were being transported on carts behind the company and were being given better food. Yet, they lost track of them. Where they were taken, what has happened to them, no one knows, and I, fluctuating between hope and desperation, keep on expecting a miracle.

In August, our friend István Havas, in whose room Ági and Pali spent their honeymoon, came home and brought a list from the Ebensee concentration camp of two hundred acquaintances who were dead. The first name on the list was Pali Radváner, our dear son-in-law, Ági's husband. He had fallen ill before Christmas and reported for admission to the hospital but they threw him out, claiming that he was just faking, and the next day, Christmas day, on the anniversary of their engagement (the day Ágnes had spent crying in Schlesiersee), he died of that "fake" illness. His old parents are waiting for him, still waiting for him…. The same list contained the name of László Hegedűs from Baja, my husband's brother, and of Miklós Wohl, the father of my niece Kató. My husband's sister Margitka – the one who had woken me up back then with news of the Germans entering Pest – was taken away along with her husband and annihilated by the Arrow Cross men. My beloved sister Erzsike, her husband, Ede, and her little stepson, Lali, ended up in the crematorium together with my dear mother.

Our family has been decimated. My heart is a bleeding wound and I often feel that I cannot bear it any more. At such times, my good son, who is trying with his devotion and tenderness to soothe my sorrow and make me forget the unforgettable, comes over and caresses me. At night, I am often awakened by the sound of János crying and shouting, tormented by nightmares. He is always dreaming about the atrocities he endured. Nothing can ever wipe away their traces, and not even a long life will make one forget – or cause to fade – the memories of the dread, the fear, the humiliation, the starvation, the freezing, the blows, the heartaches, which have soaked into our very blood. I wake him from his nightmares with tender kisses, and relief shows in his frightened eyes once he is convinced that I am there beside him. Happily clutching my hand he goes back to sleep, reassured. The knowledge that he needs me gives me the strength to carry on with life, and I know I've been sentenced to life because of him.

One time when I was anxiously waiting for the train, my fifteen-year-old niece, Kató, arrived, alone. Her loyal governess hadn't been able to walk any longer on her frozen feet and was shot. She herself had contracted typhus on the way, but she still managed to make it home, with a harrowed body that was mere skin and bones and with the memory of the crematorium in her soul. She returned home orphaned and she has become my daughter. I'm trying to replace her lost parents, I'm trying to turn her back into a schoolgirl wearing a sailor suit. But is it possible? Is there any forgetting? Can the remembrance of atrocities ever fade in one's soul?

My niece Zsófi, who had escaped weeks ahead of me and was liberated before I was, arrived home four months after me. She was kept in Lagers in Czernowitz and in Minsk for months. But she was happy, because her husband came back, too. They also found a home in my place – they are all my children, and now I have something to live for.

After all, they need some support in restarting their young lives; their faith has been shaken. I need to give them a goal in life, something necessary and worthwhile to live and struggle for: to fight against all that brought about this awful war and our terrible tragedy; to fight for a new world and for a society that does not discriminate between people on the basis of race and religion; to fight to assure that the cursed spectre of hatred will never again be resurrected; to fight for a new, happier, more beautiful life; and to prevent their children and their grandchildren from being sent into new battles as the helpless tools of the power-hungry ambitions of insane overlords.

Only a new world built on equality can compensate for the inhuman suffering and martyrdom of hundreds of thousands and millions. And only when we have accomplished this will our dear dead of holy remembrance – victims of human cruelty and madness – ever rest in peace in their graves.

Szatmár, 1945

Epilogue

After escaping the Schlesiersee death march and finding her way home, Anna almost immediately sat down to write her memoir, with the past year's experience still all-too fresh and painful in her mind. By the time her son, János, made his way home after liberation, Anna's book was almost completed and had been accepted for publication. At some point during the end of the writing process, she found out that her daughter, Ágnes, had not survived. She chose not to write about the knowledge of this tragedy in her memoir.

While Anna worked on her book, her home in Szatmár was being repaired. After the book was finished, she was able to move back into her pre-war home. During this time, Anna received a pension until, in approximately 1948, the new communist government nationalized the Industria Lemnului din Bixad, the business that her husband, Zoltán, had managed.

In 1947, Anna married a local lawyer, Andor Rosenfeld, who had lost his spouse and two young children to the gas chamber. Andor was a successful lawyer in Szatmár before and after the war. Anna and he were acquainted before the war, and reconnected after the war when they both returned to Szatmár. János, by then a freshman in college in another town, fully approved of the marriage.

As the communist party was taking over Romania, there was no future there for János, a young man of middle-class background.

With his mother no longer alone, János escaped from Romania with a view to immigrating to the United States. There, he would have the assistance of his father's former boss, who already was living in New York City. After some time in Italy awaiting permission to immigrate to the United States, János finally arrived in New York in 1949. He became a business executive in the pharmaceutical industry, married, and has two sons, one granddaughter and three grandsons.

In 1948, one of Andor Rosenfeld's clients was arrested by the communist police. Andor was also arrested, and forced to witness the torture of his client. Since he had no involvement whatsoever in the case being investigated, Andor was merely placed under house arrest. However, he never went home again. Instead, in order to save himself and Anna, he met Anna clandestinely, told her he would escape to Israel, and instructed her to apply promptly for a divorce on the grounds of abandonment. Andor, who had been a prominent Zionist, made his way to Jerusalem, from where he was able to communicate with the by-then divorced Anna through covert Zionist channels.

Soon after Andor left, Anna's home was expropriated by the communists. With no home of her own and needing to support herself, she took a course to become a dietician. Upon earning her degree she was employed by the hospital in Szatmár. Subsequently, she was transferred to Baia Mare, nearby Szatmár.

In 1950, Romania, in dire need of foreign currency, started to allow the emigration of Jews to Israel, against a fixed payment in U.S. dollars per person. Anna applied for permission to immigrate to Israel under this program and, as a single woman over the age of fifty in a non-essential occupation, she qualified for and was granted an exit visa. In this way, she was able to reunite happily with Andor in Jerusalem. Being officially divorced, Anna and Andor "lived in sin," as Anna, with her wonderful sense of humour, liked to put it.

Unfortunately, Andor's experiences during the Holocaust, followed by his second persecution and escape from Romania, took a toll on his heart; he died only one year after being reunited so happily with Anna.

Anna, now twice widowed, found herself alone in Israel, while János was attending university in New York on a student visa. Although Anna and János wished to be together again, there was no possibility of her immigrating to the United States. In order to be as close as possible, Anna decided to immigrate to Canada, where she was accepted with open arms. Anna already had relatives and even several childhood friends in Montreal, and she was able to join them there in 1952. János used his first break from university to rush up to Montreal, where he embraced his mother after five eventful and sorrowful years apart. It was a joyous reunion.

Anna, helped by her relatives and friends, settled so happily in Montreal that even once she could have immigrated to the United States after her son became a United States citizen, she nevertheless chose to remain in Canada. She became a baby nurse, staying with mothers with newborn babies for a week to several months. She adored the babies, and they and their mothers loved her and kept in touch with her long afterwards. Anna retired in 1972 at age seventy-five.

Anna was beloved by her many friends, old and new. She truly enjoyed her life in Montreal, which she termed her "third existence," after Szatmár and Jerusalem.

Despite the happiness of her "third life," her heart, as those of her beloved husbands, was also wounded by her own suffering in the 1940s and by her numerous and terrible losses. Anna died of heart failure in 1979, at the age of eighty-two, two years younger than her mother, Fanny, who died at age eighty-four in the gas chamber at Auschwitz. She was mourned by her family and her many friends. She is buried in the Mount Royal cemetery in her beloved Montreal.

Hegedűs family
2014

Glossary

antisemitism Prejudice, discrimination, persecution and/or hatred against Jewish people, institutions, culture and symbols.

Anweiserin (German; derived from the word *anweisen*, which means to direct or order) A term that was used in the Nazi camp system for a woman who was assigned a supervisory role in the barracks.

Appell (German) Roll call.

Arrow Cross Party (in Hungarian, Nyilaskeresztes Párt – Hungarista Mozgalom; abbreviation: Nyilas) A Hungarian nationalistic and antisemitic party founded by Ferenc Szálasi in 1935 under the name the Party of National Will. The party gained the full support of Nazi Germany and, renamed the Arrow Cross Party, ran in Hungary's 1939 election and won 25 per cent of the vote. The party was banned shortly after the elections but was legalized again in March 1944 when Germany occupied Hungary. Under Nazi approval, the party assumed control of Hungary from October 15, 1944, to March 1945, led by Szálasi under the name the Government of National Unity. The Arrow Cross regime was particularly brutal toward Jews, murdering approximately 20,000 between December 1944 and January 1945.

Aufseherin (German; pl. *Aufseherinnen*; female overseer or attendant) A female SS concentration camp guard.

Auschwitz (German; in Polish, Oświęcim) A town in southern Poland approximately forty kilometres from Krakow, it is also the name of the largest complex of Nazi concentration camps, which were built nearby. The Auschwitz complex contained three main camps: Auschwitz I, a slave labour camp built in May 1940; Auschwitz II-Birkenau, a death camp built in early 1942; and Auschwitz-Monowitz, a slave labour camp built in October 1942. In 1941, Auschwitz I was a testing site for usage of the lethal gas Zyklon B as a method of mass killing, which was then put into wide usage. Between 1942 and 1944, transports arrived at Auschwitz-Birkenau from almost every country in Europe – hundreds of thousands from both Poland and Hungary, and thousands from France, the Netherlands, Greece, Slovakia, Bohemia and Moravia, Yugoslavia, Belgium, Italy and Norway. More than 30,000 people were deported there from other concentration camps as well. Between May 15 and July 8, 1944, approximately 435,000 Hungarian Jews were deported to Auschwitz. It is estimated that 1.1 million people were murdered in Auschwitz; approximately 950,000 were Jewish; 74,000 Polish; 21,000 Roma; 15,000 Soviet prisoners of war; and 10,000–15,000 other nationalities. The Auschwitz complex was liberated by the Soviet army in January 1945.

Billroth batiste A waterproof medical dressing named after its developer, the Austrian surgeon Dr. Christian Albert Theodor Billroth (1829–1894).

Blockälteste (also *Blockältester*; German; literally, block elder) A prisoner appointed by the German authorities as barracks supervisor, charged with maintaining order and accorded certain privileges. Female supervisors were referred to as *Blockowa* in Polish, *Blokova* in Slovak.

Blocksperre (German; literally, "close barracks") The compulsory confinement of prisoners in their barracks. Often, inspections and selections would occur during this lockdown.

Brotkammer (German; literally, bread chamber) A place for storing bread.

Brunner, Luise A *Chef Oberaufseherin* (Chief Senior Overseer) who served at Ravensbrück and Auschwitz. After the war, Brunner was sentenced to three years' imprisonment.

Calvary (also Golgotha) A place near Jerusalem where the Christian Gospels say that Jesus was crucified.

Croesus The last king of Lydia in western Asia Minor (c. 560–546 BCE). Croesus was known for his great wealth and his name has become synonymous with riches.

Csóka, László (dates of birth and death unknown) The mayor of Satu Mare (Szatmár) during the 1944 German occupation of Hungary. Csóka participated in planning the roundup and ghettoization of the Jews of Satu Mare and its surrounding towns and cities.

Czech lager (also known as Czech Family Camp or Familienlager) A section of the Birkenau "quarantine" camp, where recent arrivals were housed temporarily, that was reserved for the more than 10,000 Czech-Jewish prisoners who were deported from the Theresienstadt camp between September and December 1943. For approximately six months, in an effort to counteract rumours that the Nazis were massacring Jews, the Czech Jews were accorded privileges such as receiving parcels and writing letters, but they were eventually subjected to the same fate as other prisoners at Birkenau. Thousands were murdered in the gas chambers on March 8 and 9, 1944; a few months later, in July, after a selection that found only a few thousand of the prisoners fit for forced labour, the rest of the family camp, more than seven thousand Czech Jews, were sent to the gas chambers.

Death's Head Also known as the *Totenkopf* (German; literally, death's head or skull), the Death's Head was one of the first combat divisions of the SS. The skull insignia was displayed on the caps or collars of the SS and the Waffen SS units. *See also* SS.

Drechsler, Margot Elisabeth (also Drexler, Dreschel; 1908–1945) A member of the SS who served at Ravensbrück concentration camp, Auschwitz and the Flossenbürg concentration camp. Drechsler received guard training at Ravensbrück in 1941, where she moved up the ranks from *Aufseherin* to *SS-Rapportführerin* (Report Overseer), a higher-ranked guard. In 1942, she was transferred to Auschwitz II–Birkenau. Drechsler worked with the notorious Josef Mengele in selecting women and children for the gas chambers and she was feared for her brutal beatings. She was executed by the Soviets in the spring of 1945. See also *Aufseherin;* Mengele, Josef.

Deutsche Wolle An abbreviated form of the name Deutsche Wollwaren Manufaktur AG (German Woolens Factory), a large textile factory located in Grünberg, Germany (now Zielona Góra, Poland), where prisoners produced fabrics used in making uniforms, army coats, parachutes and blankets. *See also* Grünberg.

Endre, László (1895–1946) The antisemitic secretary of state who headed the administrative section of the Hungarian Ministry of the Interior in 1944. Endre collaborated with the Nazis by drafting a decree that outlined the procedures to be followed and implemented in rounding up the Jewish population into ghettos and deporting Jews to concentration and death camps. After the war, Endre was tried and executed in Budapest.

FKZ (German; abbreviation of Frauen Konzentrationslager, Women's Concentration Camp) The Auschwitz FKZ was established in March 1942 with the arrival of transports of women who had been deported from Slovakia, as well as female prisoners from Ravensbrück. Transports from Hungary arrived in the women's camp at Auschwitz between May and July 1944.

Gestapo (German; abbreviation of Geheime Staatspolizei, the Secret State Police of Nazi Germany) The Gestapo were the brutal force that dealt with the perceived enemies of the Nazi regime and were responsible for rounding up European Jews for deportation to the death camps. They operated with very few legal constraints and were also responsible for issuing exit visas to the residents of German-occupied areas. A number of Gestapo members also joined the Einsatzgruppen, the mobile killing squads responsible for the roundup and murder of Jews in eastern Poland and the USSR through mass shooting operations.

ghetto A confined residential area for Jews. The term originated in Venice, Italy, in 1516 with a law requiring all Jews to live on a segregated, gated island known as Ghetto Nuovo. Throughout the Middle Ages in Europe, Jews were often forcibly confined to gated Jewish neighbourhoods. During the Holocaust, the Nazis forced Jews to live in crowded and unsanitary conditions in rundown districts of cities and towns. Hungary was divided into six military operational zones in order to facilitate the ghettoization of its Jewish population. Jews living outside of Budapest were concentrated in enclosed areas of certain cities between mid-April and May 1944. These ghettos were liquidated within a few weeks or even days, with most of the Jews deported to Auschwitz by the end of July 1944.

Grese, Irma (1923–1945) Also known as the Blond Angel of Auschwitz and the Beautiful Beast, Grese was the most notorious of SS female personnel during the war. Grese was trained as an SS guard at Ravensbrück in 1942 and transferred to Auschwitz in March 1943. In the fall of 1943, she became an *Oberaufseherin* (Senior SS-Supervisor) and was in charge of about 30,000 female Polish and Hungarian Jews. Grese was known for her brutal beatings and sadistic treatment of prisoners; she also selected prisoners for the gas chambers. After the evacuation of Auschwitz in January 1945, she was sent to Ravensbrück and was later transferred to Bergen-Belsen. Between August and November 1945, Grese was tried in the Bergen-Belsen war crimes trial in Lüneburg, Germany. She was executed in December 1945.

Gross-Rosen A village in western Poland, now named Rogoźnica, where a labour camp was established in 1940. Prisoners were forced to construct camp barracks and work in a nearby quarry. As the camp was expanded to include armaments production, Gross-Rosen became classified as a concentration camp and was the centre of a complex of at least ninety-seven sub-camps, of which Grünberg and Schlesiersee were two. As of January 1945, 76,728 prisoners were held there, of whom about one-third were women, mostly Jews. Liquidation of the sub-camps began in January 1945 and Gross-Rosen was evacuated in early February 1945, with 40,000 prisoners, including 20,000 Jews, being forced on death marches. The camp was liberated by the Soviet Red Army on February 13, 1945. It is estimated that 120,000 prisoners passed through the Gross-Rosen camp complex; 40,000 died either in Gross-Rosen or during its evacuation. *See also* Grünberg, Schlesiersee.

Grünberg (Also Gruenberg) A town and sub-camp of the Gross-Rosen concentration camp located in Lower Silesia, which had become part of Germany in 1919 and is now in western Poland. Prisoners there were forced to work in a textile factory, the Deutsche Wollwaren Manufaktur AG (German Woolens Factory), producing fabrics for military needs. Initially, German women were employed as factory workers, but their numbers decreased as increasing numbers of Jewish women from nearby towns and a camp at Neustadt were transported to Grünberg as forced labourers. The Jewish inmates worked long hours under punitive conditions and subsisted on a starvation diet. On January 29, 1945, approximately two thousand Jewish women, including prisoners from the Schlesiersee forced labour camp, were evacuated from Grünberg. Approximately half of this group was sent on a death march toward Flossenbürg concentration camp and the remainder were sent toward Bergen-Belsen concentration camp. Many died along the way of frostbite, starvation and fatigue; others were killed by SS guards for being unable to keep up or for attempting to escape. Few from either group survived the death marches. *See also* Gross-Rosen, Schlesiersee.

Häftling (German) Prison inmate.

Hasse, Elisabeth (1917–19??) An SS *Rapportführerin* (Report Leader) and *Kommandoführerin* (Work Leader) at Auschwitz from October 1942 to January 1945. Hasse was known for her savage treatment of female prisoners.

High Holidays (also High Holy Days) The autumn holidays that mark the beginning of the Jewish year and that include Rosh Hashanah (New Year) and Yom Kippur (Day of Atonement). Rosh Hashanah is observed with synagogue services, where the leader of the service blows the shofar (ram's horn), and festive meals where sweet foods, such as apples and honey, are eaten to symbolize and celebrate a sweet new year. Yom Kippur, a day of fasting and prayer at synagogue, follows ten days later.

Horthy, Miklós (1868–1957) The regent of Hungary during the interwar period and for much of World War II. Horthy presided over a government that was aligned with the Axis powers and supported Nazi ideology. After the German army occupied Hungary in March 1944, Horthy served primarily as a figurehead to the pro-Nazi government; nevertheless, he was able to order the suspension of the deportation of Hungarian Jews to death camps in the beginning of July 1944. Horthy planned to withdraw his country from the war on October 15, 1944, but the Nazis supported an Arrow Cross coup that same day and forced Horthy to abdicate.

ichthyol Ammonium bituminosulfonate, a product of oil shale rock that can be heated and processed to create a topical medicinal product for skin disorders and other purposes.

Jewish Council Also known as *Judenrat* (German) and *Zsidó Tanács* (Hungarian) A group of Jewish leaders appointed by the Germans to administer and provide services to the local Jewish population under occupation and carry out Nazi orders. The councils, which appeared to be self-governing entities but were actually under complete Nazi control, faced difficult and complex moral decisions under brutal conditions and remain a contentious subject. The chairmen had to decide whether to comply or refuse to comply with Nazi demands. Some were killed by the Nazis for refusing, while others committed suicide. Jewish officials who advocated compliance thought that cooperation might save at least some of the population; those who denounced resistance efforts did so because they believed that armed resistance would bring death to the entire community. In Hungary, some people believed that members of the Hungarian Jewish Councils were aware of the persecution and murder of Jews in various European countries but failed to warn the Jewish communities.

kapo (German) A concentration camp prisoner appointed by the SS to oversee other prisoners as slave labourers.

Labour Service (in Hungarian, *Munkaszolgálat*) Hungary's military-related labour service system that was first established in 1919 for those considered too "politically unreliable" for regular military service. After the labour service was made compulsory in 1939, Jewish men of military age were recruited to serve; however, having been deemed "unfit" to bear arms, they were equipped with tools and employed in mining, road and rail construction and maintenance work. Though the men were treated relatively well at first, the system became increasingly punitive in nature. By 1941, Jews in forced labour battalions were required to wear a yellow armband and civilian clothes; they had no formal rank and were unarmed; they were often mistreated by extremely antisemitic supervisors; and their work included clearing minefields, causing their death. Between 20,000 and 40,000 Jewish men died during their forced labour service.

Lagerälteste (German; literally, camp elder) A camp inmate in charge of the prisoner population who reported to the SS *Rapportführerin* (Report Leader).

Lagerführer (German; literally, camp leader) A senior SS officer in charge of a specific Nazi camp, the *Lagerführer* reported to the camp commandant.

Levente (abbreviation of Levente Egyesületek; Hungarian; literally, knight) A paramilitary youth corps established in Hungary in 1921. Youth between the ages of twelve and twenty-one were obliged to join the organization during World War II and underwent military training and service.

Mengele, Josef (1911–1979) The most notorious of about thirty SS garrison physicians in Auschwitz. Mengele was stationed at the camp from May 1943 to January 1945; from May 1943 to August 1944, he was the medical officer of the Birkenau "Gypsy Camp"; from August 1944 until Auschwitz was evacuated in January 1945, he became Chief Medical Officer of the main infirmary camp in Birkenau. One of the camp doctors responsible for deciding which prisoners were fit for slave labour and which were to be immediately sent to the gas chambers, Mengele was also known for conducting sadistic experiments on Jewish and Roma prisoners, especially twins.

Muselmann (German; Muslim; pl. *Muselmänner*) A slang term used by camp prisoners to describe prisoners who were near death and seemed to have lost the will to live. Some scholars attribute the use of the word Muslim to the fact that the prostrate and dying prisoners were reminiscent of devout Muslims at prayer.

Oberscharführer (German; senior squad leader) A Nazi SS party rank between 1932 and 1945. *See also* SS.

organize A Nazi camp term that meant illegally acquiring everyday objects of benefit to inmates (food, clothing, medicines, etc.).

partisans Members of irregular military forces or resistance movements formed to oppose armies of occupation. During World War II there were a number of different partisan groups that opposed both the Nazis and their collaborators in several countries. The term partisan could include highly organized, almost paramilitary groups such as the Red Army partisans; ad hoc groups bent more on survival than resistance; and roving groups of bandits who plundered what they could from all sides during the war.

Passover One of the major festivals of the Jewish calendar, Passover takes place over eight days in the spring. One of the main observances of the holiday is to recount the story of Exodus, the Jews' flight from slavery in Egypt, at a ritual meal called a seder. The name itself refers to the fact that God "passed over" the houses of the Jews when he set about slaying the firstborn sons of Egypt as the last of the ten plagues aimed at convincing Pharaoh to free the Jews.

Schlesiersee A town (present-day Sława, western Poland) that was the site of two forced labour camps, each set on a farm, during World War II. Schlesiersee was considered a sub-camp of Gross-Rosen, and the Jewish female prisoners there were forced to work for a defense company or to dig trenches. On October 22, 1944, two thousand Jewish women from Poland and Hungary were transported from Birkenau to Schlesiersee; one thousand were assigned numbers 70001 to 71000 and put to work on the eastern farm, the remainder were assigned numbers 71001 to 72000 and sent to work on the western farm under terrible conditions. The camps were evacuated on the night of January 21, 1945 and the women were sent on a death march that arrived in Grünberg on January 28, 1945, and then was forced to continue on toward the Bergen-Belsen concentration camp in northern Germany. Very few of the women survived the death march. *See also* Gross-Rosen, Grünberg.

Sonderkommando (German; special unit) Concentration camp prisoners ordered to remove corpses from the gas chambers, load them into the crematoria and dispose of the remains. On October 7, 1944, *Sonderkommando* workers coordinated an attempt to destroy the crematoria facilities at Auschwitz-Birkenau.

soubrette In opera or theatre, an archetypal, comedic female character who is coquettish or frivolous.

SS (abbreviation of Schutzstaffel; Defence Corps). The SS was established in 1925 as Adolf Hitler's elite corps of personal bodyguards. Under the direction of Heinrich Himmler, its membership grew from 280 in 1929 to 50,000 when the Nazis came to power in 1933, and to nearly a quarter of a million on the eve of World War II. The SS was comprised of the Allgemeine-SS (General SS) and the Waffen-SS (Armed or Combat SS). The General SS dealt with policing and the enforcement of Nazi racial policies in Germany and the Nazi-occupied countries. An important unit within the SS was the Reichssicherheitshauptamt (RSHA, the Central Office of Reich Security), whose responsibility included the Gestapo (Geheime Staatspolizei). The SS ran the concentration and death camps, with all their associated economic enterprises, and also fielded its own Waffen-SS military divisions, including some recruited from the occupied countries. *See also* Gestapo.

Star of David (in Hebrew, *Magen David*) The six-pointed star that is the ancient and most recognizable symbol of Judaism. During World War II, Jews in Nazi-occupied areas were frequently forced to wear a badge or armband with the Star of David on it as an identifying mark of their lesser status and to single them out as targets for persecution.

Stubendienst (German; room orderly) A prisoner in charge of maintaining the cleanliness of the block, next in command to the *Blockälteste* (barracks head). *See also Blockälteste.*

Szamos A daily political paper founded in Szatmár in 1868 that was named after the Szamos (Someş) River, which flows through Szatmár. The paper was fairly liberal before World War I and published the work of numerous well-known Hungarian writers, but became right-wing under the direction of editor-in-chief Albert Figus in October 1940. Figus turned the paper into a Christian nationalist political daily, antisemitic in nature. The paper ceased publication in 1944 after Figus's death.

Tantalus A son of Zeus in Greek mythology who is punished for a variety of crimes, including stealing ambrosia and nectar, the foods of the gods, to give to mortals. As punishment, Tantalus is kept within reach of water he cannot eat and food he cannot drink, and a large stone hangs over his head, ready to fall.

Vertreterin (German; representative) Deputy barracks chief.

Vorarbeiter (German; foreman) A work crew chief or senior worker.

Waschraum (German; pl. *Waschräume*) Washroom; lavatory.

Yiddish A language derived from Middle High German with elements of Hebrew, Aramaic, Romance and Slavic languages, and written in Hebrew characters. Spoken by Jews in east-central Europe for roughly a thousand years from the tenth century to the mid-twentieth century, it was still the most common language among European Jews until the outbreak of World War II. There are similarities between Yiddish and contemporary German.

Photographs

1 Anna Hegedűs's father, Henrik Molnár. Szatmár, date unkown.

2 Fanny Moskovits, Anna's mother, as a young woman.

3 Molnár family portrait. Standing, Anna's brother Lászlo. Seated, left to right: sister Margit, brother Ödön, and mother, Fanny; Anna; Anna's father, Henrik, and sisters Iren and Erzsike. Szatmár, circa 1905.

Wedding photo of Anna and Zoltán Hegedűs, 1921.

1 Anna and her son, János, at six months. January 21, 1928.
2 Anna's daughter, Ágnes, age five. Circa 1928.
3 Zoltán and János, circa 1939.
4 Ágnes, age fifteen, dressed up for her first dance. Szatmár, 1938.

1

2

1 The Hegedűs family at their holiday home. Left to right: Anna, János, Ágnes, Zoltán and Anna's niece Zsófi. Bikszád, circa 1935.

2 Zoltán, János, Anna and Ágnes, circa 1937.

Anna and Zoltán in St. Mark's Square, Venice.

The family celebrating Anna Hegedűs's mother's eightieth birthday. Seated: Anna's sister Erzsike (left) and their mother, Fanny. Standing, left to right: János, Zoltán, Veronique, Anna, Ágnes, Lászlo and Lali. Bikszád, April 24, 1940.

Ágnes, 1943.

1 Ágnes's fiancé, Pali Radváner, wearing his labour service uniform prior to his
deportation. Date unknown.
2 Ágnes and Pali. April 1943.

1 János, approximately age twenty, in Milan, Italy, after the war. 1948.
2 Anna, age fifty-one, in Nagybánya, Hungary after the war. 1948.
3 Anna and János on the occasion of their first reunion in North America. Montreal, November 28, 1952.
4 Anna Hegedűs. Montreal, 1957.

Anna Molnár Hegedűs. Montreal, 1969.

Index

The Azrieli Foundation

The Azrieli Foundation was established in 1989 to realize and extend the philanthropic vision of David J. Azrieli, C.M., C.Q., M.Arch. The Foundation's mission is to support a wide spectrum of initiatives in education and research. The Azrieli Foundation is an active supporter of programs in the fields of Education, the education of architects, scientific and medical research, and the arts. The Azrieli Foundation's many initiatives include: the Holocaust Survivor Memoirs Program, which collects, preserves, publishes and distributes the written memoirs of survivors in Canada; the Azrieli Institute for Educational Empowerment, an innovative program successfully working to keep at-risk youth in school; the Azrieli Fellows Program, which promotes academic excellence and leadership on the graduate level at Israeli universities; the Azrieli Music Project, which celebrates and fosters the creation of high-quality new Jewish orchestral music; and the Azrieli Neurodevelopmental Research Program, which supports advanced research on neurodevelopmental disorders, particularly Fragile X and Autism Spectrum Disorders.